Life's Short, Quiz Hard.

Dr. Coff E. Koffi-Coffy

Life's Short, Quiz Hard.
An Unofficial *Gilmore girls* Trivia Book

SIMON ELEMENT
New York   Amsterdam/Antwerp   London
Toronto   Sydney/Melbourne   New Delhi

An Imprint of Simon & Schuster, LLC
1230 Avenue of the Americas
New York, NY 10020

This book is not endorsed by or affiliated with the network or the producers.

For more than 100 years, Simon & Schuster has championed authors and the stories they create. By respecting the copyright of an author's intellectual property, you enable Simon & Schuster and the author to continue publishing exceptional books for years to come. We thank you for supporting the author's copyright by purchasing an authorized edition of this book.

No amount of this book may be reproduced or stored in any format, nor may it be uploaded to any website, database, language-learning model, or other repository, retrieval, or artificial intelligence system without express permission. All rights reserved. Inquiries may be directed to Simon & Schuster, 1230 Avenue of the Americas, New York, NY 10020 or permissions@simonandschuster.com.

Copyright © 2025 by Simon & Schuster UK Ltd.

All rights reserved, including the right to reproduce this book or portions thereof in any form whatsoever. For information, address Simon Element Subsidiary Rights Department, 1230 Avenue of the Americas, New York, NY 10020.

First Simon Element trade paperback edition November 2025

SIMON ELEMENT is a trademark of Simon & Schuster, LLC

Simon & Schuster strongly believes in freedom of expression and stands against censorship in all its forms. For more information, visit BooksBelong.com.

For information about special discounts for bulk purchases, please contact Simon & Schuster Special Sales at 1-866-506-1949 or business@simonandschuster.com.

The Simon & Schuster Speakers Bureau can bring authors to your live event. For more information or to book an event, contact the Simon & Schuster Speakers Bureau at 1-866-248-3049 or visit our website at www.simonspeakers.com.

Interior design by Jaime Putorti

Manufactured in the United States of America

1 3 5 7 9 10 8 6 4 2

Library of Congress Control Number has been applied for.

ISBN 978-1-6682-3008-4 (pbk)
ISBN 978-1-6682-3009-1 (ebook)

Contents

Introduction	ix
Gilmore Haste, Less Speed	1
Season 1	7
Lorelai and Max	15
Home Sweet Home	19
Emily Gilmore	23
I Like Big Books and I Cannot Lie	29
Season 2	31
Rory and Dean	39
Luke's Diner	43
Richard Gilmore	47
Striking a Chord	51

Season 3	57
Lorelai and Christopher	65
The Dragonfly and Independence Inn	69
Taylor Doose	73
(Gilmore) Girls on Film	77
Season 4	81
Rory and Jess	89
Stars Hollow Festivals and Events	93
Lane Kim	95
Nobody Puts Rory in the Corner	99
Season 5	105
Lorelai and Luke	113
Chilton	117
Kirk Gleason	121
Food Glorious Food	125
Season 6	129
Rory and Logan	137
Yale	141
Paris Geller	145
Sookie St. James	149

Season 7	153
Random Dates	161
Extra-Curricular	165
Luke Danes	169
Friday Night Dinners	173
Christopher Hayden	175
A Year in the Life	179
Answers	197

Introduction

Welcome to the *Gilmore girls* trivia book, a place where, unlike actual life, you get the answers given to you on page 197.

The story of a mother and daughter finding their way with a little help from their friends has been comforting us for twenty-five years. Now, it's time to re-live the cosy, heart-warming, quip-laden masterpiece through the medium of quiz.

Over seven (OK, eight, with the revival) seasons and more than 150 hours, *Gilmore girls* is a joyous celebration of the small things that matter most. And now, you can compete over who remembers most of them.

Whether you're someone who has barely scratched the surface, or is on your 25th deep dive, there's something here for everyone.

So grab a coffee. Grab two coffees. Heck, if legal, grab a glass of wine. And get ready to take a quizzing

LIFE'S SHORT, QUIZ HARD.

adventure in . . . we nearly just totally gave away the answer to question six.

Stop reading this, turn the page and let the fun begin.

Because, believe it or not, some people can live a hundred years without really quizzing a minute.

Gilmore Haste, Less Speed

Right, before we get going, let's test some of the basics. There's no point trying to run a marathon before you can crawl, after all. By the end of the book you'll be a world expert in *Gilmore girls*, but let's start with the quizzing equivalent of a gentle walk.

Here are twenty easy ones to get you going.

1. Although Lorelai and her parents have a strained relationship, Emily and Richard agree to pay for Rory to go to an expensive prep school on which one condition?
    a: Lorelai must find a new job
    b: Lorelai and Rory must move in with them
    c: Lorelai and Rory must attend dinner at their house every Friday
    d: Rory must get straight As in school

LIFE'S SHORT, QUIZ HARD.

2. How old was Lorelai when she gave birth to Rory?
    a: 16
    b: 17
    c: 18
    d: 20

3. How old is Rory when the series starts?
    a: 14
    b: 15
    c: 16
    d: 17

4. What is Rory's real name?
    a: Victoria
    b: Rosanna
    c: Lorelai
    d: Mallory

5. What is the name of Rory's absent father?
    a: Michel Gerard
    b: Kirk Gleason
    c: Taylor Doose
    d: Christopher Hayden

GILMORE HASTE, LESS SPEED

6: In which town has Lorelai lived since leaving home?
   a: Stars Hollow
   b: Hartford
   c: New Milford
   d: Mystic

7: In which state is the show set?
   a: New York
   b: Connecticut
   c: Massachusetts
   d: Rhode Island

8: Where did Lorelai find a job to support herself and Rory once she left her parents' house?
   a: At the grocery store, working as a cashier
   b: At Luke's Diner, working as a waitress
   c: At the Independence Inn, working as a maid
   d: At the beauty supply shop, working as a sales assistant

9: From the time Rory was born to the start of the series, Lorelai and Rory would visit Emily and Richard on specific occasions. Which ones?
   a: Richard and Emily's birthdays
   b: Rory and Lorelai's birthdays
   c: Christmas, Thanksgiving and Easter
   d: Halloween and Independence Day

LIFE'S SHORT, QUIZ HARD.

10: Who is Rory's best friend?
    a: Louise Grant
    b: Madeline Lynn
    c: Lane Kim
    d: Patricia LaCosta

11: What does Lorelai's best friend Sookie St. James do for a living?
    a: She is a florist
    b: She is a chef
    c: She is a hairdresser
    d: She is a teacher

12: What is Lorelai's ultimate career goal?
    a: To own her own restaurant
    b: To own her own bar
    c: To own her own bookstore
    d: To own her own inn

13: Who is the owner of the diner?
    a: Luke Danes
    b: Christopher Hayden
    c: Kirk Gleason
    d: Taylor Doose

GILMORE HASTE, LESS SPEED

14: Which Ivy League university has Rory always wanted to go to from a young age?
   a: Yale
   b: Harvard
   c: Princeton
   d: Columbia

15: How many seasons of *Gilmore girls* are there?
   a: 4
   b: 6
   c: 7
   d: 9

16: In which year did the series first air in the US?
   a: 1999
   b: 2000
   c: 2001
   d: 2003

17: When was the finale to the series shown in the US?
   a: 2006
   b: 2007
   c: 2008
   d: 2010

LIFE'S SHORT, QUIZ HARD.

18: In what year was the revival released and what was it called?
    a: 2015, *Gilmore girls: Taking the Next Step*
    b: 2016, *Gilmore girls: A Year in the Life*
    c: 2017, *Gilmore girls: On My Own*
    d: 2018, *Gilmore girls: Return to Stars Hollow*

19: How many episodes were there in the revival and what were they named after?
    a: There were four episodes, each named after one of the four seasons
    b: There were six episodes, each named after a show location
    c: There were ten episodes, each named after a character on the show
    d: There were twelve episodes, each named after a month of the year

20: Who is the creator of *Gilmore girls*?
    a: Daniel Palladino
    b: Amy Sherman-Palladino
    c: Josh Schwartz
    d: Mark Schwahn

Season 1

To everything there is a season and *Gilmore girls* took the decision to begin their journey with Season 1. Originally broadcast on 5 October 2000, when the *New York Times* greeted it as 'likable if lightweight', many worried about how it would fare in its US timeslot up against some show called *Friends*.

SEASON 1

1: Which local public school does Rory leave to go to Chilton prep school?
  a: Hartford High
  b: Stars Hollow High
  c: Weston High
  d: Choate Rosemary Hall

2: What grade does Rory get on her first English assignment at Chilton?
  a: A
  b: B
  c: C
  d: D

3: In which episode does Rory first meet Dean Forester at the grocery store?
  a: Episode 1, 'Pilot'
  b: Episode 2, 'The Lorelais' First Day at Chilton'
  c: Episode 3, 'Kill Me Now'
  d: Episode 4, 'The Deer Hunters'

4: Rory had two parties on consecutive nights to celebrate her 16th birthday. Where were they? (Choose two answers)
  a: At her grandparents'
  b: At Luke's Diner
  c: At her house in Stars Hollow
  d: At the Independence Inn

LIFE'S SHORT, QUIZ HARD.

5: Who told Lorelai about Rory's first kiss with Dean?
 a: Paris
 b: Lane
 c: Kirk
 d: Mrs Kim

6: Where is Lorelai when Rory's teacher, Max Medina, first asks her out on a date?
 a: Parents' evening
 b: A bake sale at Chilton
 c: A coffee shop
 d: In her car

7: When Rory is snowed in at her grandparents' house and they are without a cook, what do they eat?
 a: Chinese takeout
 b: Spaghetti Bolognese
 c: Frozen pizza
 d: Hot dogs

8: Who does Dean refuse to fight with at the Chilton formal?
 a: Jess
 b: Luke
 c: Tristan
 d: Logan

SEASON 1

9. Can you solve the following riddle to find the joyful cameo is this season?

   My first is in join but not in onion
   My second is in orchestrate but not in threescore
   My third is in politician but not in topical
   My fourth is in convenient but not in convict
   My first is in girdle but not in ridge
   My second is in secrecy but not in cress
   My third is in censure but not in secure
   My fourth is in incriminate but not in entertainment
   My fifth is in leash but not in sale

10: Who drives Lorelai to the hospital after Richard has a heart attack at Christmas?
   a: Christopher
   b: Luke
   c: Max
   d: Rory

11: What is Lorelai studying at community college?
   a: Business
   b: Hospitality
   c: French
   d: Journalism

LIFE'S SHORT, QUIZ HARD.

12: Christopher arrives in Stars Hollow in Episode 15. How many times before this has he visited the town?
 a: 0; this is his first time
 b: 16 times; once a year since they moved there
 c: 32 times; twice a year since they moved there
 d: Too many to count

13: Why do Rory and Dean break up in Season 1?
 a: Dean was jealous about Rory's relationship with Tristan
 b: Rory wanted to focus on her schoolwork
 c: Dean was upset that he told Rory 'I love you' and she didn't feel ready to say it back
 d: Lorelai did not approve of the relationship

14: When Emily is shown around Stars Hollow by Rory, she is shocked by Rory and Lorelai's old living quarters. Where did they used to live?
 a: In a room at Miss Patty's School of Ballet
 b: Above the diner
 c: With Kirk and his mother
 d: A tool shed at the Independence Inn

SEASON 1

15: When Rory finds out Max and Lorelai are back together, she is really upset. Where does she run away to?

    a: Lane's house
    b: Her grandparents' house
    c: Luke's Diner
    d: Dean's house

16: What does Luke's girlfriend, Rachel, say to Luke when she leaves town for good?

    a: That she hates Lorelai
    b: That she doesn't want a life running the diner
    c: Not to wait too long to tell Lorelai how he feels
    d: That she has met someone else

Lorelai and Max

Romeo and Juliet. Jack and Rose. Ross and Rachel. To that pantheon, we can add Lorelai and Max. Sort of. Their relationship might have been short and sweet, taking place essentially over a few intense weeks, but, like Danny DeVito covered in cupcake frosting, once experienced, it's not something anyone involved is going to forget.

1: What subject does Max teach at Chilton?

2: Lorelai is unsure about going on a proper date with Max but agrees to meet him for what beverage?

LIFE'S SHORT, QUIZ HARD.

3: Which book does Max lend Lorelai that she finally admits to giving up reading?
    a: *Moby-Dick* by Herman Melville
    b: *Swann's Way* by Marcel Proust
    c: *Ulysses* by James Joyce
    d: *To the Lighthouse* by Virginia Woolf

4: Which student finds Lorelai and Max kissing in a classroom during the school day?
    a: Paris
    b: Madeline
    c: Louise
    d: Henry

5: When Max says he dated a little during their breakup in Season 1, and he accuses Lorelai of dating Luke, what does she tell him?
    a: That she was too upset to date
    b: That her mother set her up on a date at Friday Night Dinner
    c: That she slept with Rory's dad on her parents' balcony
    d: That they were broken up so it's none of his business

LORELAI AND MAX

6: What does Max send to Lorelai after she says his marriage proposal should be more than an attempt to end bickering?

    a: 100 yellow daisies
    b: 500 yellow daisies
    c: 1,000 yellow daisies
    d: 10,000 yellow daisies

7: Where was Max's job the summer before the wedding?

8: A long while after Lorelai and Max's wedding is called off, a present arrives at Lorelai's house. What is it?

    a: An ice-cream maker
    b: A blender
    c: A microwave
    d: An expensive vase

9: Can you solve this anagram to find the state where Max has been when he and Lorelai meet up again in Season 3?

AFRICAN OIL

Home Sweet Home

Smallville, Hawkins, Indiana, Derry, Maine – some towns just become iconic, and *Gilmore girls*' fictional Connecticut town of Stars Hollow is arguably one of the most important characters in the show.

1: What is the name of the grocery store in Stars Hollow?

2: What is the population of Stars Hollow?
   a: 9,971
   b: 9,973
   c: 9,975
   d: 9,977

3: Which Stars Hollow store does Mrs Kim own?

LIFE'S SHORT, QUIZ HARD.

4: What is Miss Patty's School of Ballet sometimes used for?

5: What happened after the failed romance between the flower and candy store owners?

6: What did Old Man Twickham leave to the town?

7: Can you solve this anagram to discover which vehicle-related feature is introduced to the town for the first time in Season 2?

   GLITCH TARIFFS

8: Why does the town smell of rotting eggs after the Easter egg hunt?

9: What change is made to the annual Battle of Stars Hollow reenactment?
   a: It takes place at night
   b: It is rewritten as a musical
   c: A woman's role is included for the first time
   d: It is performed twice in one day

HOME SWEET HOME

10: Babette and Miss Patty organise a party in Season 5 that is a first for the town. What is it?
   a: An Avon party
   b: A Tupperware party
   c: A Botox party
   d: A clothes-swapping party

Emily Gilmore

Lorelai's mother, Emily Gilmore, is a real high-society lady who lives in a world of comfortable privilege. Although a little chilly and guarded, and always keen to be in control, she is a strong, independent woman whose love for her granddaughter Rory burns brightly.

1: To help her understand the internet, Richard shows Emily the website of one of her favourite fashion houses. Which one?
   a: Louis Vuitton
   b: Hermès
   c: Yves Saint Laurent
   d: Gucci

LIFE'S SHORT, QUIZ HARD.

2: Lorelai tells Rory that in an interview that was meant to be about the Dragonfly Inn, the interviewer asked about her relationship with Emily. What did Lorelai call her mother?
   a: The female Hitler
   b: The female Pol Pot
   c: The female Stalin
   d: The female Mussolini

3: What does Emily tell Richard after he has his heart attack in Season 1?
   a: That she couldn't believe Christmas had been ruined
   b: That she was so scared she couldn't manage the drive to the hospital
   c: That Rory had been a huge comfort to her
   d: That he is not allowed to die before her

4: How does Emily hear about Max and Lorelai's engagement?
   a: Lorelai tells her at Friday Night Dinner
   b: She receives a written invitation from Lorelai
   c: Sookie invites her to the surprise engagement party
   d: Richard tells her over the phone as soon as he finds out

EMILY GILMORE

5: Which popular Stars Hollow location did Emily describe to Luke and Lorelai as 'very charming' and 'nice and rustic' at their first Friday Night Dinner together after they start dating?
  a: Mrs Kim's antiques shop
  b: Independence Inn
  c: Dragonfly Inn
  d: Luke's Diner

6: When Dean beeped the car horn to pick up Rory for the Chilton dance instead of getting out of the car and coming to the door, how did Emily respond?
  a: She did not allow Rory to leave the house
  b: She exclaimed that Rory was not fried chicken and that the house wasn't a drive-thru
  c: She stated that chivalry was now dead
  d: She blamed Lorelai for letting Rory date a hooligan

7: After Emily and Richard separate, Emily goes on a date with Simon McLane. What does she do when she gets home afterwards?
  a: She bursts into tears
  b: She calls Richard because she realises she misses him
  c: She fires the maid for a silly reason
  d: She calls Simon to say she had a fabulous time

LIFE'S SHORT, QUIZ HARD.

8: Why does Emily invite Christopher to her and Richard's vow renewal?

9. How does Lorelai describe Emily's signature scent?

10: Can you solve the following riddle to find the destination Rory and Emily went to together for the summer?

> My first is in contentiousness but not in suction
> My second is in retouch but not in hector
> My third is in staircase but not in ascetic
> My fourth is in integration but not in tangerine
> My fifth is in implant but not in militant
> My sixth is in great but not in ragtag

11: Where does Emily have her bachelorette party the night before the vow renewal?

12: How does Emily react when Rory moves out of the pool house and back to Stars Hollow?
   a: She tries to buy a plane
   b: She tries to buy a Porsche
   c: She tries to buy a summer house
   d: She fires the maid

EMILY GILMORE

13: Emily gives Shira Huntzberger a real dressing down for the way she treated Rory. When she later tells the family about the incident, what does she wish she had remembered to call Shira?
  a: Poor
  b: A trophy wife
  c: A bad mother
  d: A cocktail waitress

I Like Big Books and I Cannot Lie

Hundreds of books are featured in the *Gilmore girls* world. In particular, Rory's love of literature is an important part of her journey throughout the show – an interest she shares with Luke's nephew, Jess.

All of the following books were seen in the show, but which character was reading them – Jess or Rory?

1. *A Room of One's Own* by Virginia Woolf

2. *The Unabridged Journals of Sylvia Plath*

3. *A Confederacy of Dunces* by John Kennedy Toole

4. *The Electric Kool-Aid Acid Test* by Tom Wolfe

LIFE'S SHORT, QUIZ HARD.

5. *Visions of Cody* by Jack Kerouac

6. *The Divine Comedy: Volume 1: Inferno* by Dante

7. *One Hundred Years of Solitude* by Gabriel García Márquez

8. *Atonement* by Ian McEwan

9. *Northanger Abbey* by Jane Austen

10. *A Heartbreaking Work of Staggering Genius* by Dave Eggers

Season 2

On 9 October 2001, Season 2 of *Gilmore girls* was broadcast, and if anything, the 'banter dial' was turned up even higher. There have been reports that scripts for *Gilmore girls* were 15–20 pages longer than other shows due to the sheer volume of fast-paced dialogue.

SEASON 2

1: Sookie throws Lorelai a bachelorette party before her wedding to Max. Who does Lorelai call afterwards?
   a: Christopher
   b: Luke
   c: Rory
   d: Emily

2: What does Luke make for Lorelai and Max's wedding?
   a: A seating plan sign
   b: Bunting
   c: A chuppah
   d: Table centrepieces

3: When Lorelai runs away with Rory before her wedding, where do they go?
   a: Yale
   b: Harvard
   c: Atlantic City
   d: New York

4: When Luke's nephew, Jess Mariano, first arrives in Stars Hollow, what does he steal from Babette?
   a: Car keys
   b: A jewellery box
   c: Cash
   d: A garden gnome

LIFE'S SHORT, QUIZ HARD.

5: Who escorts Rory at her debutante ball?
    a: Richard
    b: Christopher
    c: Lorelai
    d: Dean

6: For a school assignment, Rory plays Juliet in Act 5 of *Romeo & Juliet*. Who plays Romeo in the final performance?
    a: Paris
    b: Tristan
    c: Henry
    d: Madeline

7: How does Lorelai get the $15,000 to pay for the termite damage to her house?
    a: She remortgages the house
    b: Luke loans her the money
    c: Richard gives her the cash she needs
    d: Emily co-signs a loan from the bank

8: Can you solve this anagram to find the iconic musical cameo in Season 2?

GENIAL CORK

SEASON 2

9: Who outbids Dean at the basket auction in order to have lunch with Rory?
   a: Tristan
   b: Jess
   c: Lane
   d: Dave

10: Christopher introduces his girlfriend to Rory and Lorelai this season. What is her name?
   a: Nicole
   b: Anna
   c: Sherry
   d: Rachel

11: How does Rory fracture her wrist?
   a: Falling outside the diner with her mother
   b: In a wheelbarrow accident with Kirk
   c: Bumping into another student at the Chilton cafeteria
   d: In a car accident with Jess

12: Jess goes back to New York and Rory goes to see him. What reason does she give him for coming?
   a: That she argued with her mother
   b: That she misses him
   c: That he left without saying goodbye
   d: That Luke wants him to come home

LIFE'S SHORT, QUIZ HARD.

13: Rory is devastated that she misses an important event when she is delayed coming back from New York. Which one?
　　a: Her mother's graduation
　　b: Her grandparents' wedding anniversary
　　c: Sookie's engagement
　　d: Lane's birthday

14: Why does Lorelai start to avoid having breakfast in Luke's Diner?
　　a: Luke has stopped serving coffee
　　b: She has argued with Luke over Jess
　　c: She prefers Sookie's breakfast
　　d: She has argued with Luke over Rachel

15: At what event does Rory kiss Jess, even though she is still with Dean?
　　a: Lorelai's birthday
　　b: Lane's graduation
　　c: Sookie's wedding
　　d: The Stars Hollow Summer Carnival

SEASON 2

16: In the season finale, Lorelai and Christopher have a night together at the Inn and tell Emily and Rory they are getting back together. Why does Christopher end up leaving and disappointing Lorelai again?

    a: His girlfriend calls and says she is pregnant
    b: His girlfriend calls and says she wants him back
    c: Rory tells him to leave her mother alone
    d: Rory tells him she doesn't want him in her life

Rory and Dean

We all remember our first love, and Dean – sweet, available, reliable, boy next door that he is – was solid first boyfriend material for Rory, even if he sometimes became jealous and was eventually left behind. I mean, come on, he even said 'I love you' first!

1: Where did Dean live before his move to Stars Hollow?
   a: LA
   b: New York
   c: Hartford
   d: Chicago

2: What did Dean make Rory for her 16th birthday present?

LIFE'S SHORT, QUIZ HARD.

3: What did Rory say to Dean after their first kiss in the grocery store?
    a: 'Thank you'
    b: 'I love you'
    c: 'That was a surprise'
    d: 'I think the customers are looking'

4: Where do Rory and Dean go to hang out and then end up falling asleep for the night after leaving the Chilton formal?

5: Can you solve this anagram to find the author that Dean read on Rory's recommendation?

    NAUSEATE NJ

6: Which anniversary are Rory and Dean celebrating when she is allowed to miss Friday Night Dinner?

7: What does Rory finally tell Dean in the Season 1 finale?

8: How does Rory let Dean know about the car accident she was in with Jess?

9: When Rory asks Dean to pick her up after a bad date at Yale, who are they surprised by at her dorm?

RORY AND DEAN

10: When is the last time we see Dean in the series (before his appearance in the revival)?
   a: At his sister's graduation
   b: Begging Lindsay to take him back
   c: Warning Luke about how hard it is to date a Gilmore Girl
   d: Apologising to Lorelai for the affair with Rory

Luke's Diner

Sometimes you just want to go where everybody knows your name. Simple, no frills but utterly cosy, Luke's Diner is always there with a milkshake or a burger and fries – or just gallons and gallons of coffee. You know that whatever else is going on in life, the diner will be there, the still point of the spinning Stars Hollow universe.

1: There's a big sign behind the counter at Luke's Diner. What does it say?
    a: 'No Amex'
    b: 'No credit'
    c: 'No cell phones'
    d: 'No laptops'

LIFE'S SHORT, QUIZ HARD.

2: Can you solve this anagram to discover what the diner was when Luke's dad owned it?

ARROWHEAD TEARS

3: When Luke goes fishing and closes the diner, where does Lorelai have to go for coffee?
   a: Weston's bakery
   b: The Hungry Diner
   c: The Independence Inn
   d: Nowhere; she buys a coffee machine

4: What did the diner host the morning after the fire at the Independence Inn?

5: When Luke is dating Nicole, what change does he make to the menu on her advice?
   a: He includes more sandwich options
   b: He adds more tea varieties
   c: He adds more salads
   d: He expands the dessert menu

6: How do Lorelai and Rory get people to give up their tables in the diner?
   a: They hover right behind them
   b: They get Luke to move them
   c: They ask Kirk to sit with them
   d: They act crazy around them

LUKE'S DINER

7: Why do the town residents decide to boycott the diner and eat at Weston's?

8: What did Luke have to cook in the diner for his sister's Renaissance Fayre wedding?

9: What can you sometimes get Luke to put in the mud pie served at the diner?
   a: Hershey's Kisses
   b: Sour Patch Kids
   c: Oreos
   d: Gummy Worms

10: What is the name of the diner cook?

Richard Gilmore

Rory's grandfather is a successful businessman and classic patriarch. Polished and polite, he values duty, responsibility and reputation. This means he can sometimes find it hard to understand Lorelai's choices, but he is a proud, doting grandfather.

1: Can you solve this riddle to find the university that Richard went to?

My first is in player but not in repeal
My second is in snakelike but not in skinless
My third is in lightning but not in night
My fourth is in hothouse but not in shout

2: Which character is introduced by Richard as 'Lorelai the first'?

LIFE'S SHORT, QUIZ HARD.

3: Richard is unhappy that Dean has given Rory a car, so he asks Gypsy to check it for faults. What does she find?
   a: Malfunctioning windscreen wipers
   b: Dodgy brakes
   c: Nothing is wrong with it
   d: It won't start

4: What news does Richard reveal at the Bracebridge Dinner that upset Emily but explained why he was so happy?
   a: He has retired
   b: He has taken up golf
   c: He is going to Europe for work
   d: He has been secretly meeting Christopher

5: Where did Richard propose to Emily?

6: Which a cappella group did Richard sing with at university?

7: Richard comes out of retirement to go into business with Jason Stiles. Who is he?

RICHARD GILMORE

8: How long was Richard naked for during his sophomore year at Yale?
   a: 1 hour
   b: 1 day
   c: 1 week
   d: 1 month

9: Who is Pennilyn Lott?

10: What happens when Richard finds out about Emily and Simon from his colleagues and sees them together?
   a: He punches Simon
   b: He moves into a hotel
   c: He crashes his car into hers
   d: He begs Emily to take him back

11: What does Richard bring to Lorelai to start the conversation about getting Rory back to Yale?

12: What does Richard teach at Yale in Season 7?

13: Richard used to hate radishes but now likes them. What caused the change?
   a: He now salts them
   b: His doctor recommended he eat them
   c: He fell off a horse
   d: Sookie cooks them in a special way

Striking a Chord

Whether it's the soundtrack to Rory and Lorelai's quickfire dialogue, Lane's musical journey or part of a festival, music in *Gilmore girls* is a constant presence and adds hugely to the tone of the show. And, honestly, who among us hasn't wished that musician Sam Phillips could produce one of her trademark sparse guitar riffs for a key moment in our own lives?

1: Lorelai and Sookie take Rory and the Chilton girls to which girl group's concert?
   a: Bananarama
   b: The Spice Girls
   c: The Bangles
   d: The Go-Go's

LIFE'S SHORT, QUIZ HARD.

2: Can you solve this anagram to uncover Christopher's favourite band?

FRIGHTEN FOPS

3: Tristan offers which singer's concert tickets to Rory?
   a: Jewel
   b: Britney Spears
   c: Fiona Apple
   d: PJ Harvey

4: Which album does Rory buy her mother as a graduation present?
   a: *Different Light* by The Bangles
   b: *Beauty and the Beat* by The Go-Go's
   c: *Parallel Lines* by Blondie
   d: *Crimes of Passion* by Pat Benatar

5: When Lane first meets Dave, he knows she is a musician because of which band t-shirt she is wearing?
   a: The Clash
   b: Ramones
   c: Dead Kennedys
   d: Misfits

STRIKING A CHORD

6: What song does Lorelai listen to when she is waiting to give birth to Rory?
    a: 'Take On Me'
    b: '99 Luftballons'
    c: 'I Ran'
    d: 'Tainted Love'

7: Which Clash song do the band play in their first rehearsal in the music shop?
    a: 'Rock the Casbah'
    b: 'The Guns of Brixton'
    c: 'I Fought the Law'
    d: 'London Calling'

8: After Rory and Dean sleep together, which song does Rory want to be 'their song'?

9: Can you solve these anagrams to find bands who appeared as buskers in Season 6, Episode 22?

ELTON GOYA + CHOOSY UNIT

10: Which musician does Mrs Kim use as an example for Lane's band as someone who doesn't swear, mentions God and made $57 million last year?

LIFE'S SHORT, QUIZ HARD.

11: Which Blondie song do Hep Alien cover in the last gig of their church tour at the Whitfield Seventh Day Adventist Church gym?
    a: 'Hanging on the Telephone'
    b: 'Atomic'
    c: 'Rapture'
    d: 'Heart of Glass'

12: The episode 'Just Like Gwen and Gavin' refers to which two singers?

13: Which band do Zach and Lane pose as on their wedding cake?
    a: Fleetwood Mac
    b: The White Stripes
    c: Sonic Youth
    d: ABBA

14: Which artist hired the town troubadour to open for him?
    a: Bruce Springsteen
    b: Bob Dylan
    c: Neil Young
    d: Elvis Costello

STRIKING A CHORD

15: Which Bon Jovi song do the Whiffenpoofs cover?
a: 'Always'
b: 'Shot Through the Heart'
c: 'Blaze of Glory'
d: 'Living on a Prayer'

16: Zach plays an acoustic version of which Celine Dion ballad at Michel's dog, Chin-Chin's, funeral?

17: Which Whitney Houston hit is Lorelai singing at karaoke when Luke walks in?

18: Who are the four members of Hep Alien after Dave leaves?

Season 3

The Godfather. Lord of the Rings. Star Wars (for a bit) . . . *Gilmore girls* entered the fabled ranks of the trilogy on 24 September 2002, when Season 3 was broadcast, and it's fair to say it dramatised a big year in the Gilmore house . . .

SEASON 3

1: The season opens with Lorelai having a surprising dream. What was it?
    a: She was married to Christopher and Rory had a brother
    b: She met Paul Anka
    c: She lived with Luke and was pregnant with twins
    d: Rory graduated from Harvard top of her class

2: Who does Rory initially want to write her Harvard admissions essay about?
    a: Hillary Clinton
    b: Christiane Amanpour
    c: Sylvia Plath
    d: Ruth Bader Ginsburg

3: Lane starts secretly dating Dave Rygalski. How do they first meet?
    a: At detention at school
    b: He is looking for a drummer
    c: In the Stars Hollow music shop
    d: A blind date

4: Who devil-egged Jess's car?
    a: Babette and Miss Patty
    b: Dean
    c: Kirk and Taylor
    d: Rory and Lorelai

LIFE'S SHORT, QUIZ HARD.

5: Dean finally admits the obvious attraction between Jess and Rory and breaks up with Rory very publicly. Where does the break-up take place?
 a: The Battle of Stars Hollow reenactment
 b: The 24-hour dance marathon
 c: The Winter Carnival
 d: The Stars Hollow nativity

6: Emily and Richard take Rory and Lorelai to Yale university. What has Richard organised as a surprise?
 a: A guided tour of his student haunts
 b: A performance of his singing group
 c: An admissions interview for Rory
 d: A formal dinner with current students and alumni

7: In a 1984 flashback, how did Lorelai let her parents know she was in labour?
 a: She leaves them a note
 b: She calls them on the phone
 c: She shouts from her bedroom
 d: She leaves Christopher to tell them

8. Can you solve this anagram to discover the actor who appeared in the show before leaving, presumably, for more sunshine and vitamins?

BODY DRAMA

SEASON 3

9: What is the name of Christopher's baby, and Rory's half-sister?
   a: Gia
   b: Mia
   c: Gigi
   d: Fifi

10: Rory is furious when Jess turns up to Friday Night Dinner with a black eye. How did he get it?
   a: He got in a fight with Dean outside the grocery store
   b: A swan attacked him
   c: Luke accidentally banged into him in the diner
   d: He was in a motorbike accident

11: What was the clue that Sookie was pregnant?
   a: She was shouting at everyone in the kitchen
   b: She went off vegetables
   c: She cooked terrible-tasting food
   d: She was nauseous

LIFE'S SHORT, QUIZ HARD.

12: Which three Ivy League universities did Rory get into?
    a: Columbia
    b: Dartmouth
    c: Harvard
    d: Yale
    e: Brown
    f: Cornell
    g: Princeton

13: In the same episode that Jess leaves Stars Hollow for California, Dean tells Rory something about his relationship with Lindsay, his new girlfriend. What is it?
    a: They are engaged
    b: They have broken up
    c: She is pregnant
    d: They have eloped

14: Lorelai pays her parents back for the Chilton loan, but Rory then asks them to pay for her Yale tuition. Why?
    a: She doesn't want to burden her mother financially
    b: She wants her mother to be able to renovate her house
    c: She wants her mother to be able to buy the Dragonfly Inn
    d: She didn't realise how much the tuition would be

SEASON 3

15: Where do Rory and Lorelai go on holiday after she graduates?
    a: A girls' trip to Vegas
    b: An all-inclusive hotel in the Caribbean
    c: A staycation in Stars Hollow
    d: Backpacking around Europe

16: In the season finale, what does Luke dream about Lorelai?
    a: That she is pregnant with twins
    b: That she tells him not to get engaged to Nicole
    c: That she is waiting for him at the altar of their wedding
    d: That they are dancing together

Lorelai and Christopher

Lorelai's first serious boyfriend, and Rory's father, Christopher has remained a presence in both their lives. Though their teen romance was intense, it ended when Lorelai became pregnant and made the decision to raise Rory on her own. He often seems to represent a 'path not taken' moment for Lorelai, and his involvement as a father swings between engagement and distance over the course of the show.

1: What vehicle does Christopher arrive on when he makes his first appearance in the series?

LIFE'S SHORT, QUIZ HARD.

2: What does Christopher buy Lorelai as a present for her graduation?
    a: A framed photo of Lorelai, Rory and himself
    b: Nothing; he forgot
    c: A gift basket that includes a real pearl necklace
    d: A fruit basket

3: In the 1984 flashback, in the hospital when Rory is born, Christopher says Rory is pretty. Lorelai corrects him and says she is . . .
    a: Noisy
    b: Perfect
    c: Lovely
    d: Beautiful

4: After Emily reconciles with Richard in Season 5, she goes to Boston to say what to Christopher?
    a: He needs to get a proper job
    b: He needs to take more responsibility for Rory
    c: He needs to finally apologise to her and Richard
    d: He needs to fight for Lorelai

LORELAI AND CHRISTOPHER

5: When Christopher and Lorelai start dating again in Season 7, they do a lot of movie dates. What film is particularly disappointing?
   a: *Snakes on a Plane*
   b: *Mission Impossible III*
   c: *The Prestige*
   d: *Final Destination III*

6: Why do Christopher and Lorelai go to Paris?

7: When they are jetlagged in Paris and can't sleep but are starving, what does Christopher do for Lorelai?

8: Lorelai and Christopher have a romantic time in Paris. How does Christopher address her on their return?
   a: 'Baby mama'
   b: 'Fiancée'
   c: 'Girlfriend'
   d: 'Mrs Hayden'

9: What are the signs that Christopher mentions that showed Lorelai was not into their marriage?

The Dragonfly and Independence Inn

The Independence Inn provided a home for Lorelai and Rory when they first arrived in Stars Hollow and introduced us to fan favourites Sookie and Michel. Sookie and Lorelai finally got their independence from the inn when they bought the Dragonfly and achieved their long-held dream of owning their own business.

1: What was the name of the owner of the Independence Inn who took in Lorelai and a baby Rory?

2: How do Lorelai and Sookie find out about the Dragonfly Inn?

3: Who is the owner of the Dragonfly Inn who won't sell to Sookie and Lorelai?

LIFE'S SHORT, QUIZ HARD.

4: Who plays the part of Squire Bracebridge at the Bracebridge Dinner?
    a: Jackson
    b: Luke
    c: Taylor
    d: Kirk

5: Where is Lorelai when she gets the call that the Independence Inn is on fire?

6: Who loans Lorelai the $30,000 needed to finish the Dragonfly Inn renovations?

7: On what object did Lorelai write the details of the first reservation at the Dragonfly Inn?
    a: Michel's new reservations book
    b: A Post-it note
    c: The new computer booking system
    d: A Big Red chewing gum wrapper

8: Who does Michel want to invite to the Dragonfly Inn test run?

THE DRAGONFLY AND INDEPENDENCE INN

9: When Michel wins the gameshow *The Price Is Right*, his prize is delivered to the Inn. What is it?
 a: A motor home
 b: A motor boat
 c: A microwave
 d: A mixer

10: Can you solve this anagram to discover the magazine that interviews Lorelai about the Dragonfly Inn?

CAMEL NARRATIVE

11: When Taylor wants to change the Stars Hollow street names back to their historical ones, what are Lorelai and the rest of the staff dismayed to find out was the name of Dragonfly Inn's street?
 a: Third Street
 b: Sores and Boils Alley
 c: Honeypot Lane
 d: Peach Street

Taylor Doose

Equal parts earnest and utterly absurd, Taylor is essentially Stars Hollow in human form. Never one not to enforce a rule, he is often at loggerheads with Luke and other residents, but it always comes from a place of love and care.

1: Which new arrival to Stars Hollow did Taylor consider a 'hooligan' and call a Town Hall meeting about?

2: What type of shop does Taylor open in Season 4?

3: What do the town residents find funny about Taylor's appearance when he returns from holiday?
   a: He is sunburnt
   b: He has a whole new wardrobe
   c: He has a mismatched toupee
   d: He is wearing glasses

LIFE'S SHORT, QUIZ HARD.

4: Taylor brought a motion at the Town Hall about whether Luke and Lorelai should be allowed to start dating. Did he vote for or against the relationship?

5: Who does Taylor lose the Selectman election to (by a massive landslide) in Season 5?
   a: Jackson
   b: Kirk
   c: Luke
   d: Morey

6: Why does Taylor give the town residents pink or blue ribbons to choose from?

7: When Taylor is stuck in Maine, who takes over the organisation of the Winter Carnival?
   a: Jackson
   b: Kirk
   c: Luke
   d: Morey

8: Taylor installs a camera at the red light in town. What happens at his demonstration of how it works?
   a: The traffic lights fail
   b: Kirk crashes into the traffic light
   c: Kirk crashes his car into Luke's Diner
   d: No one shows up to the demonstration

TAYLOR DOOSE

9: What is the reason that Taylor gives for the town smelling like pickles?
   a: A train derailed nearby
   b: A lorry overturned nearby
   c: The diner over-ordered pickles
   d: Kirk has set up a pickling business

(Gilmore) Girls on Film

Gilmore girls is chock full of references to film and television. Not only is this one of the key ways that Rory and Lorelai relate, but their mother-and-daughter movie nights (with snacks a-plenty!) are a treasured ritual.

1: Which film does Lorelai invite Dean to come and watch for his first visit to their house?
   a: *Pippi Longstocking*
   b: *Willy Wonka & the Chocolate Factory*
   c: *Babe*
   d: *Annie Hall*

LIFE'S SHORT, QUIZ HARD.

2: After Rory gets excellent PSAT scores, they plan to dress up and see which film to celebrate?
 a: *The Rocky Horror Picture Show*
 b: *Grease*
 c: *Harry Potter and the Philosopher's Stone*
 d: *The Wizard of Oz*

3: Rory spots two young boys looking at the cover of an inappropriate film in the video shop, leading Taylor to put films rated above a G behind a red curtain. Which film were the boys looking at?
 a: *Sliver*
 b: *The Blue Lagoon*
 c: *Basic Instinct*
 d: *Showgirls*

4: Taylor shows the same film for the town's movie night every year because it is the best one they can project for free. Which film is it?
 a: *Little Women*
 b: *The Grapes of Wrath*
 c: *The Yearling*
 d: *Old Yeller*

(GILMORE) GIRLS ON FILM

5: Which film series do Lorelai and Rory want to watch before she leaves for Yale?
   a: The *Lord the Rings* trilogy
   b: The original *Star Wars* trilogy
   c: The *Matrix* trilogy
   d: The *Godfather* trilogy

6: Which film has Luke never seen until he watches it with Lorelai on a movie night?
   a: *Casablanca*
   b: *The Maltese Falcon*
   c: *The African Queen*
   d: *Angels with Dirty Faces*

7: Which Merchant Ivory film do Lorelai and Rory watch after Rory gets home from her trip to Europe with Emily?
   a: *Howards End*
   b: *A Room with a View*
   c: *The Remains of the Day*
   d: *Maurice*

LIFE'S SHORT, QUIZ HARD.

8: When Lorelai is upset after her breakup with Luke, she watches which original film and its remakes with Sookie?
    a: *Love Affair*
    b: *Freaky Friday*
    c: *A Star Is Born*
    d: *Seven Samurai*

9: Paris hasn't managed to sleep through the night since seeing which film as a child?
    a: *Chitty Chitty Bang Bang*
    b: *The Wizard of Oz*
    c: *Carrie*
    d: *A Nightmare on Elm Street*

10: Which film did Lorelai and Sookie want to watch for Lane's bachelorette party?
    a: *American Gigolo*
    b: *Pretty Woman*
    c: *An Officer and a Gentleman*
    d: *Indecent Proposal*

11: Which film does Lorelai show at April's birthday party?
    a: *Ferris Bueller's Day Off*
    b: *The Breakfast Club*
    c: *Weird Science*
    d: *Pretty in Pink*

Season 4

John, Paul, George and Ringo! It's time for fab Season 4 of *Gilmore girls*. Broadcast on 23 September 2003, it was greeted warmly by fans, who welcomed their beloved characters leaving their comfort zones. Note: Please do not try to match Lorelai coffee for coffee in this season. You will die.

SEASON 4

1: Lorelai and Rory have a week's worth of activities planned before Rory starts at Yale, but it turns out Rory got the dates wrong and they only have two days. How do they spend Rory's last night together?
    a: Having Friday Night Dinner at the grandparents'
    b: Ordering every single item on the menu at Luke's Diner
    c: Having their favourite main courses cooked by Sookie at the Inn
    d: Having dinner at their house with all their friends from Stars Hollow

2: Why is Luke embarrassed about what happened on his cruise with Nicole?
    a: She disembarked halfway through
    b: They broke up before the boat sailed
    c: They got married and now they are getting divorced
    d: They got sick of each other

3: Which Chilton student surprised Rory in her suite at Yale on her first day?
    a: Tristan
    b: Madeline
    c: Louise
    d: Paris

LIFE'S SHORT, QUIZ HARD.

4: Rory's first weekend trip back to Stars Hollow accidentally coincides with which event she would probably rather miss?
    a: Jess's book launch
    b: Dean's wedding
    c: Taylor's birthday
    d: Kirk and Lulu's first date

5: Why are the town residents worried about letting Lorelai be the Renoir girl in the Festival of Living Pictures?
    a: She flinched last time
    b: She sneezed last time
    c: She coughed last time
    d: She laughed last time

6: What is Emily outraged to find out at the Yale–Harvard football match?
    a: Rory doesn't like football
    b: The Yale mascot is a dog
    c: Richard sees his ex-girlfriend once a year
    d: They have to attend a tailgating party

SEASON 4

7: Richard has a new business partner, Jason, who is very interested in Lorelai, but she is concerned about her parents' reaction. Why does Lorelai finally accept his invitation to go on a date?
    a: She likes the flowers and candy he sends her
    b: She has a big argument with her mother
    c: Rory tells her to enjoy herself
    d: Her dad says he approves

8: Can you solve this anagram to discover the actor who appears as a cameo in this season before finding himself a new girl?

A FEDEX GREMLIN

9: Why does Mrs Kim tell Lane that she should move out?
    a: Lane wants to work in Luke's Diner
    b: Lane doesn't want to go to church anymore
    c: She doesn't approve of Lane mixing with boys
    d: Lane wants to be a drummer and practice with her band

LIFE'S SHORT, QUIZ HARD.

10: What does Jess say to Rory on a quick visit back to Stars Hollow before driving away?
   a: 'I belong in New York'
   b: 'I love you'
   c: 'Tell Luke I'm sorry'
   d: 'Say hi to your mum for me'

11: Why does Emily refuse to help with her mother in law Trix's funeral?
   a: She found a letter Trix wrote to Richard telling him not to marry Emily
   b: Trix didn't leave her anything in her will
   c: She was too busy looking after a grieving Richard
   d: She didn't see eye to eye with Lorelai over the arrangements

12: On Spring Break, who do Louise and Madeline make Rory drunkenly leave a voicemail for?
   a: Jess
   b: Tristan
   c: Dean
   d: Henry

SEASON 4

13: When Richard betrays Jason by taking all their clients to Jason's father, why does Lorelai break up with Jason?
    a: Because she blames him for the business falling apart
    b: Because her father will disown her if she doesn't
    c: Because she doesn't want to disappoint Rory
    d: Because she can't be with someone who is suing her family

14: How do Lorelai and Rory find out that Emily and Richard have separated and Emily is staying in a hotel?
    a: The maid lets it slip when she answers the door
    b: Richard whispers the truth to them in the kitchen
    c: They see her leave the house after Friday Night Dinner
    d: They hear Emily on the phone when they are waiting for dinner

15: After listening to a self-help audiotape and workbook about finding love, what does Luke realise?
    a: He needs to love himself first
    b: He needs to apologise to Jess
    c: He should forgive his sister Liz
    d: He loves Lorelai

LIFE'S SHORT, QUIZ HARD.

16: When does Luke finally ask out Lorelai?
    a: When he is opening the diner and Lorelai comes for coffee
    b: After his sister's wedding
    c: While his sister and TJ are saying their vows
    d: At the Dragonfly Inn test run

Rory and Jess

In the same way as you might get bored of the same old pizza you always order, after Dean, Rory goes for something with SPICE to change things up. Rory and Jess connect over literature, music and being sarcastic about things, but along with that comes an emotional unavailability that Rory finds difficult to handle.

1: What does Jess draw outside of Doose's Market?

2: Jess wins Rory's food basket in the charity auction, so they have lunch together. What does Rory leave behind that Jess keeps?

3: Where are Jess and Rory driving back from when they have their car accident?

LIFE'S SHORT, QUIZ HARD.

4: When Rory goes to New York to see Jess, she knows she can find him at his reading spot. Where is it?
  a: Washington Square Park
  b: The Empire State Building
  c: A cafe near Times Square
  d: The New York Public Library

5: Who is Jess's girlfriend that Rory is extremely jealous of in Season 3?

6: Dean tries to start a fight with Jess after he sees him kissing Rory. Why does Jess refuse to fight him?
  a: He doesn't do fights
  b: Rory will think it's his fault
  c: He is going to meet Rory
  d: He promised Luke he wouldn't get into any more fights

7: Can you solve the following anagram to discover the actress who appeared in cameos playing two separate characters, including Jess's father's girlfriend?

FRY HEN LINENS

RORY AND JESS

8: Can you solve this riddle to find where Jess was working when he won employee of the month?

   My first is in brow but not in orb
   My second is in cantor but not in contort
   My third is in dreadful but not in defraud
   My fourth is in transmitter but not in restrainer
   My fifth is in teaspoon but not in stepson
   My sixth is in frost but not in soft
   My seventh is in conceitedness but not in indecision

9: Who does Jess visit when he leaves Stars Hollow to go to California?
   a: His friend who has just moved there
   b: His mother, Liz
   c: His cousin who will give him a job
   d: His father, Jimmy

10: What does Jess ask Rory when he turns up at Yale?

11: What does he say has changed?
   a: She can count on him now
   b: He has grown up and is ready
   c: He has a regular income
   d: He has repaired his relationship with his parents

LIFE'S SHORT, QUIZ HARD.

12: What is the title of the book that Jess wrote?

13: What is the name of the publishing house that Jess works at and Rory visits in Philadelphia?

Stars Hollow Festivals and Events

Maybe there are loads of town festivals where I live and nobody tells me, but in Stars Hollow they are a big deal. It can sometimes feel that not a week goes by without some local event occurring, bringing all of the town's characters together in maximum quirk mode.

Put the following events in the correct month:

1. Battle of Stars Hollow reenactment   January

2. Stars Hollow holiday pageant/nativity   November

3. Festival celebrating the founding
   of Stars Hollow   March

4. Poe Festival   January

LIFE'S SHORT, QUIZ HARD.

5. First Annual Stars Hollow End of
   Summer Madness Festival   December

6. 24-hour Dance Marathon   August

7. Winter Carnival   November

Solve the anagrams for three more Stars Hollow events:

8. AFFLICTION PIGLETS SURVIVE

9. EMPIRICAL LADDER

10. AM BLAZE, YEAH

Lane Kim

Rory's best friend, Lane Kim is always there to support Rory. But she also has her own journey as she struggles to balance her strict, religious upbringing with her own hopes and dreams, most notably her intense passion for rock music.

1: Lane was really unhappy with the outcome of her career aptitude test. Which career did she get?
   a: Finance
   b: Teaching
   c: Sales
   d: Insurance

2: Who does Lane meet at Madeline's party, which causes her to worry that she is falling for someone her parents would approve of?

LIFE'S SHORT, QUIZ HARD.

3: Can you solve this anagram to discover the lab partner that Lane had to keep secret from Rory?

FEET ADORNERS

4: Dave Rygalski and Lane have their first kiss on which holiday?

5: When a music shop opens up in Stars Hollow, Lane discovers which instrument?

6: What is the name of Lane's band?

7: What colour does Rory dye Lane's hair, before she quickly dyes it back?
    a: Purple
    b: Red
    c: Blue
    d: Pink

8: Can you solve this anagram to discover the Bohemian actor who plays a student at Lane's college in Season 4?

KARLA MIME

LANE KIM

9: Why is the diner one of Mrs Kim's approved places for Lane to work?
   a: Mrs Kim wants her to learn how to cook
   b: Mrs Kim trusts Luke
   c: No alcohol is served and it's within walking distance of a church
   d: Mrs Kim knows most of the customers

10: Who is Mrs Kim shocked to find out Lane is living with when she first visits Lane in her new place?

11: Where was Lane and Zach's first date?
   a: Their living room
   b: The diner
   c: The Black, White and Read movie theatre
   d: A Town Hall meeting

12: What does Lane say she is risking by being in a band?
   a: Her soul
   b: Eternal damnation
   c: Her relationship with her mother
   d: Her relationship with Zach

LIFE'S SHORT, QUIZ HARD.

13: How many wedding ceremonies does Lane have when she marries Zach?
    a: 1
    b: 2
    c: 3
    d: 4

14: When did Rory and Lane first meet?
    a: At birth
    b: In kindergarten
    c: In first grade
    d: In second grade

Nobody Puts Rory in the Corner

Gilmore girls is famous for its pop culture references, a crucial part of Lorelai and Rory's trademark fast-paced patter.

1: Which pop star's video did Rory think she was going to be in when she first saw her Chilton uniform?

2: Rory says Paris's parents' divorce is more sordid than which celebrity's scandal?
  a: Hugh Grant
  b: Monica Lewinsky
  c: George Michael
  d: Prince Charles

LIFE'S SHORT, QUIZ HARD.

3: When Christopher wants to marry Lorelai in Season 1, Lorelai thinks this is so crazy he would freak out which notorious cult leader?
    a: Jim Jones
    b: Charles Manson
    c: Marshall Applewhite
    d: David Koresh

4: Lorelai compares sleeping with Christopher on her parents' balcony to two disasters combined. Which ones?
    a: Chernobyl
    b: The Hindenburg
    c: Space Shuttle *Challenger*
    d: The *Titanic*

5: Who does Madeline think was the Courtney Love of her day?
    a: Elizabeth Taylor
    b: Marilyn Monroe
    c: Judy Garland
    d: Jayne Mansfield

6: When Luke is making noise fixing her house, who does Lorelai compare him to?
    a: Mariah Carey
    b: Guns N' Roses
    c: Foo Fighters
    d: Blue Man Group

NOBODY PUTS RORY IN THE CORNER

7: Who does Bootsy say gets a gland from a pig's head shot in their rear end to keep them looking young?
    a: Ivana Trump
    b: Donald Trump
    c: Ivanka Trump
    d: Barron Trump

8: On their road trip to Harvard, which celebrity Harvard graduate is Lorelai impressed by?
    a: Eddie Munster (Butch Patrick)
    b: Morticia Addams (Carolyn Jones)
    c: Herman Munster (Fred Gwynne)
    d: Gomez Addams (John Astin)

9: What does Jess call Dean and Rory kissing in the store?
    a: A 'Leonardo and Clare moment'
    b: A 'vertical *From Here to Eternity* moment'
    c: A 'Hans Solo and Princess Leia moment'
    d: A '*Gone with the Wind* moment'

10: When Lorelai is getting ready for her graduation and sneezes near a chalkboard, who does she liken herself to?
    a: Robin Williams in *Good Will Hunting*
    b: Russell Crowe in *A Beautiful Mind*
    c: Woody Allen in *Annie Hall*
    d: Harrison Ford in *Indiana Jones*

LIFE'S SHORT, QUIZ HARD.

11: Paris asks Rory to run for student vice-president and says she is looking for the . . .
    a: 'Ryan to my Hanks'
    b: 'Damon to my Affleck'
    c: 'De Niro to my Pacino'
    d: 'Winslet to my DiCaprio'

12: When Dave comes to see Lane at the 24-hour Dance Marathon, what does he compare the event to?
    a: *Mulholland Drive*
    b: *Twin Peaks*
    c: *Blue Velvet*
    d: *Lost Highway*

13: When Jess walks away from Dean who is trying to fight him, he says it is getting a bit too . . .
    a: *Fight Club*
    b: *Karate Kid*
    c: *Rambo*
    d: *West Side Story*

14: Whose advice does Sherry follow to squat when in labour?
    a: Howard Stern
    b: Ricki Lake
    c: Dr Benjamin Spock
    d: Martha Stewart

NOBODY PUTS RORY IN THE CORNER

15: Which South Park impression can Lorelai do?
   a: Stan
   b: Kenny
   c: Cartman
   d: Mr Garrison

Season 5

Five fingers on each hand, five toes on each foot, five senses and from 21 September 2004 five seasons of *Gilmore girls*. This series marks a gear change as the highs are higher with Luke and Lorelai finally together, but the lows are lower for Rory in her second year at Yale. Though, I suppose mathematically that means the middle still stays where it is.

SEASON 5

1: How does Lindsay find out about Rory and Dean's affair?
   a: She sees them kissing
   b: Kirk tells her by accident
   c: She finds a letter in Dean's jacket
   d: Dean confesses when she confronts him

2: After spending the night with Luke, Lorelai accidentally reveals their new relationship by doing what?
   a: Walking down into the diner wearing only his shirt
   b: Kissing him behind the counter
   c: Telling Miss Patty and Babette
   d: Waving at Taylor out of Luke's bedroom window

3: When Richard moves into the pool house and Emily stays in the main house, how do he and Emily divide Friday Night Dinner with Lorelai and Rory?
   a: They have the main meal with Emily and dessert with Richard
   b: They have the cocktails and starter with Emily and the main meal with Richard
   c: They have the wine and cheese with Richard and the main meal with Emily
   d: They have the soup with Richard and the main meal with Emily

LIFE'S SHORT, QUIZ HARD.

4: Luke and Lorelai have their first double date that is so awkward it ends in a game of Bop It. Who is it with?
    a: Sookie and Jackson
    b: Rory and Dean
    c: Kirk and Lulu
    d: Babette and Morey

5: After Sherry leaves Christopher, Christopher calls Lorelai for help with Gigi. Why does Rory tell Christopher to stay away from her mother?
    a: It upsets Lorelai to see Christopher looking after a baby
    b: He needs to learn how to be a single father
    c: He only calls when he needs something from them
    d: She is in a relationship with Luke now

6: Dean and Rory break up when Dean realises he doesn't belong in her world anymore. Where does the break-up happen?
    a: At her grandparents' house
    b: Luke's Diner
    c: Miss Patty's School of Ballet
    d: Her room at Yale

SEASON 5

7: Emily and Richard celebrate getting back together with a vow renewal and a celebration for which wedding anniversary?
   a: 25th
   b: 30th
   c: 35th
   d: 40th

8: Can you solve this anagram to discover the literary cameo that appeared in this season?

MARLIN MOANER

9: What sparks a big argument between Luke and Christopher at the vow renewal?
   a: Emily seats them next to each other
   b: They both want to dance with Lorelai
   c: They find Logan and Rory kissing
   d: Luke is jealous that Richard wants to talk business with Christopher

LIFE'S SHORT, QUIZ HARD.

10: Why does Lorelai tell her mother that the relationship between the two of them is done?
- a: Emily throws Luke out
- b: Christopher reveals that Emily wants Lorelai with him instead of Luke
- c: Rory says that Emily invited Christopher to split up Luke and Lorelai
- d: Richard says that Emily invited Christopher because Lorelai should get back together with him

11: After Logan and Rory agree to date exclusively, Rory meets Logan's family, who think she is unsuitable for him. How does Logan's father apologise for the family's behaviour?
- a: He offers to get her an interview at Condé Nast
- b: He invites her to their summer house in the Hamptons
- c: He offers her an internship at one of his newspapers
- d: He asks her to come back for dinner where his wife will say sorry

SEASON 5

12: Why isn't Sookie able to attend the baby shower Lorelai and Rory want to throw for her?
   a: She is in labour
   b: She is working late at the Inn
   c: It was a surprise party and they forgot to tell her about it
   d: She is snowed in

13: What does Rory do when she is told she doesn't have what it takes for journalism at the end of her internship?
   a: She goes back to Stars Hollow in tears
   b: She steals a boat and ends up in jail
   c: She crashes her car into Luke's Diner
   d: She stays at Yale over the summer to take extra classes

14: When Lane tells her mother the band isn't working out, what does Mrs Kim do?
   a: Organises a band tour of churches over the summer
   b: Tells her it's time to move back home
   c: Offers to get her more music lessons
   d: Says it was her fault for getting involved in rock 'n' roll

LIFE'S SHORT, QUIZ HARD.

15: Lorelai asks for her parents' help in stopping Rory from dropping out of Yale. Why is she surprised at the following Friday Night Dinner?
    a: Richard and Emily don't let her in the house to attend Friday Night Dinner
    b: Richard and Emily announce Rory is going to take a gap year in Europe
    c: Richard and Emily tell Lorelai that they can't help and she will have to sort the problem out herself
    d: Richard and Emily announce Rory will move into their pool house and take time off from Yale

16: Lorelai proposes to Luke in the last scene of the season. What does Luke say in response?
    a: Nothing
    b: 'Why?'
    c: 'What?'
    d: 'Are you serious?'

Lorelai and Luke

You know that thing in a rom com where two characters meet and immediately hate each other – like he's the president of Dog Inc. and she's the leader of the local cat appreciation club or something, and it's so obvious that they're going to get together? Well, *Gilmore girls* does NOT do that with Lorelai and Luke.

Luke and Lorelai and their slow, winding relationship of near misses, all backgrounded by deep bonds of friendship and trust, is arguably the emotional core of the show. Who doesn't want their 'I'm all in' moment?!

1: How does Lorelai first hear about Luke's ex-girlfriend Rachel?
   a: Jess tells Rory about her
   b: She sees a photo of her at the diner
   c: She accidentally buys her old sweater
   d: Luke's sister mentions her

LIFE'S SHORT, QUIZ HARD.

2: How does Luke work out that Lorelai is dating Jason?
 a: She was never dressed weather-appropriate
 b: She always had a smile on her face
 c: She stopped drinking coffee
 d: She did her hair differently

3: Where do Lorelai and Luke have their first date?
 a: The diner after opening hours
 b: Sniffy's Tavern
 c: Friday Night Dinner
 d: Weston's Bakery

4: On the first day that Lorelai and Luke met, Lorelai gave Luke something that he kept in his wallet. What was it?

5: How long did he keep it?
 a: 2 years
 b: 4 years
 c: 6 years
 d: 8 years

6: Who was Lorelai with the night before the Stars Hollow Battle reenactment and didn't tell Luke?

LORELAI AND LUKE

7: Where does Luke go when he is upset after hearing about Emily's plan to get Christopher and Lorelai back together?
 a: To the cinema
 b: Fishing on his own
 c: To see Jess in Philadelphia
 d: To see his sister

8: Why don't Lorelai and Luke set a date after Lorelai proposes?

9: When Lorelai's house renovation is finished, Luke surprises her by installing his grandmother's bedroom set. How does Lorelai react?
 a: She gets straight into bed
 b: She loves it
 c: She thinks it is old and creepy
 d: She doesn't notice

10: What date does Lorelai choose for their wedding after she finds her perfect dress?
 a: 3rd June
 b: 3rd July
 c: 3rd August
 d: 3rd September

LIFE'S SHORT, QUIZ HARD.

11: What is Luke's main reason for not getting married?
    a: He wants to build a relationship with Rory first
    b: He doesn't think Lorelai is over Christopher
    c: April is now in his life
    d: He wants her parents to approve of him

12: Where does Lorelai tell Luke that she and Christopher got married in Paris?
    a: At the hospital
    b: At the diner
    c: At the grocery store
    d: In the town square

13. What does Luke tell Lorelai before they kiss in the series finale?
    a: He never stopped loving her
    b: He just wants to see her happy
    c: He forgives her
    d: He organised Rory's party to get Lorelai back

Chilton

This elite private prep school is a real change of pace from Stars Hollow. Academically rigorous, strict and demanding, Lorelai can only send Rory there because her parents agree to pay the fees. At first a source of rivals and then friends, it plays a key part in Rory's early journey in the show.

1: In which town is Chilton located?

2: Which animal does Rory crash into on her way to her English exam on Shakespeare?

3: What colour is Rory's school backpack?

4: What is the name of the Chilton student newspaper?

LIFE'S SHORT, QUIZ HARD.

5: What is the name of the leading secret society at Chilton?

6: When Rory and Paris win the school presidential election, which surprise group voted for them?
    a: The school band
    b: The debate team
    c: The AV club
    d: The jocks

7: Rory finishes her freshman year in the top what percentage of her class?
    a: 1%
    b: 3%
    c: 5%
    d: 10%

8: Which subjects is Rory taking at the Chilton summer school?
    a: Shakespeare, physics and obscure Russian poetry
    b: Maths, English literature and chemistry
    c: History, geography and French novellas
    d: Biochemistry, further maths and music

9: Headmaster Charleston is concerned about Rory's social interactions with other students outside of class. What does the Chilton guidance counsellor ask Rory not to do at lunchtime?

CHILTON

10: Lorelai also gets criticised for her lack of involvement with the school. Which group does she end up joining after pressure from her mother?

11: How does Lorelai find out that Rory is valedictorian of her class?

Kirk Gleason

Ironically, one of the few professional roles Kirk never holds is any sort of captain. But he is a fixture of Stars Hollow and his regular appearances displaying his latest hobby or obsession are a constant quirky feature of town life throughout the show.

Match Kirk's job to the season:

1. Tow truck operator – Season 1

2. Wrapping paper salesman – Season 2

3. Termite inspector – Season 3

4. Dog walker – Season 4

5. Mailman Season – 5

LIFE'S SHORT, QUIZ HARD.

6. Assistant manager at Doose's Market – Season 6

7. Winter Carnival coordinator – Season 7

8: Why does Kirk install an alarm in Lorelai's house without asking?
    a: There has been a spate of burglaries in Stars Hollow
    b: He is worried about her living alone
    c: Taylor has mandated it for the town
    d: He wants an example of his work to show other customers

9: Who does Kirk start dating in Season 4?

10: Kirk is overjoyed to be cast as Jesus in the Last Supper tableaux in the Festival of Living Pictures, but ends up fighting with which other biblical figure?
    a: Matthew
    b: Thomas
    c: Peter
    d: Judas

11: Which star part does Kirk play in the Battle of Stars Hollow reenactment?

KIRK GLEASON

12: What animal is Kirk scared of?
   a: Goldfish
   b: Cats
   c: Mice
   d: Monkeys

13: What does Paris say that Kirk talks about in his sleep?
   a: Roulette
   b: Poker
   c: Blackjack
   d: Craps

Food Glorious Food

Whether it's Pop Tarts or pizza, Chinese takeout or a Sookie St. James special, food is a big deal in Stars Hollow. It's something that binds the characters together, like an egg, and yet mealtimes are often where conflicts and tensions play out. From the structured high class Friday Night Dinners to the relaxed space of the Inns or diner, food is an expression of the different sorts of love, connection and community that fill the show.

1: What does Luke cook Lorelai to make her feel better when Rory goes to her grandparents' Christmas party in Season 1?
　a: Reindeer pancakes
　b: A Santa burger
　c: Santa's elves cookies
　d: A Christmas tree sandwich

LIFE'S SHORT, QUIZ HARD.

2: What shape doughnuts does Rory bring for Halloween in Season 1?
   a: Ghosts
   b: Pumpkins
   c: Clowns
   d: Cats

3: What is Sookie's famous breakfast, served at Luke's after the fire at the Inn?
   a: Country breakfast skillet
   b: Biscuits and sausage gravy
   c: French toast, bacon and maple syrup
   d: Blueberry-lemon pancakes, Bananas Foster and Belgian waffles

4: What does Rory cook for Dean dressed as Donna Reed?
   a: Steak, greens and mashed potato
   b: Burger, fries and coleslaw
   c: A hot dog and potato salad
   d: Fried chicken, red beans and rice and gravy

5: What does Sookie make for Lorelai's graduation?
   a: A cake with her photo on it
   b: A blueberry pie
   c: A tassel hat cake
   d: Four different types of cake

FOOD GLORIOUS FOOD

6: On Lorelai's 35th birthday, Rory gives her the 'world's largest pizza'. How does she transport it?

7: What does Lorelai want her 35th birthday cake to say?
    a: 'Happy 16th Birthday, Lorelai'
    b: 'Happy 18th Birthday, Lorelai'
    c: 'Happy 30th Birthday, Lorelai'
    d: 'Happy 35th Birthday, Lorelai'

8: What does Mrs Kim bring to Lane the first time she visits her in her new place?
    a: Soy pudding
    b: Rice cakes
    c: Honey pastries
    d: Shaved ice

9: What type of cake do Lorelai and Michel usually eat when they plan the tasks for the handyman at the Inn?
    a: Vanilla cupcakes
    b: Chocolate fudge cake
    c: Carrot cake
    d: Red velvet cake

LIFE'S SHORT, QUIZ HARD.

10: What is the 'Rory' cocktail served at Rory's 21st birthday?
    a: Champagne and mango puree
    b: Champagne, orange juice and cranberry juice
    c: Champagne, vodka, pineapple juice and grenadine
    d: Champagne in a special Rory glass

Season 6

In the Book of Revelations (which was actually the working title for this book), the number six is associated with the devil. But it also the first 'perfect' number in number theory. So, it's no surprise that Season 6 of *Gilmore girls*, broadcast on 13 September 2005, is a series of contrasts. Some have found the twists the characters are dealt somewhat troubling, while others are unbothered by the fact that the stakes are higher. Like a tall butcher.

SEASON 6

1: How many hours of community service does Rory get sentenced to for stealing the boat?
   a: 100
   b: 200
   c: 300
   d: 400

2: When Rory goes to the diner after her first day of community service, what is she shocked to find out from Luke?
   a: He and Lorelai are engaged
   b: Her mother has left town on a solo trip
   c: Taylor held a vote to see if Luke and Lorelai should date
   d: Lane has moved back home

3: Lane reveals to the band that she has secretly saved up their earnings from the church tour. How much did they earn?
   a: Over $3,000
   b: Over $6,000
   c: Over $9,000
   d: Over $12,000

LIFE'S SHORT, QUIZ HARD.

4: How does Sookie try to get Lorelai and Rory talking again?
- a: She makes them their favourite cake and invites them round
- b: She asks them both to be godmothers to her children
- c: She pretends that each of them has asked to meet the other
- d: She won't return to work if they don't start talking again

5: When Rory finally moves out of her grandparents' pool house, where does she go?
- a: Lane's
- b: Yale
- c: Her mother's
- d: Paris's

6: April turns up at the diner and takes a photo of Luke and a hair from his head for a science project. What is her project?
- a: Testing for hair dye
- b: Analysing hair growth
- c: A DNA test
- d: Checking for wigs

SEASON 6

7: Christopher comes back to Stars Hollow with an inheritance he would like to share with Rory and Lorelai. What does Rory want the money for?
   a: To pay her grandparents back for Chilton
   b: Her Yale tuition
   c: A holiday with Lorelai
   d: A downpayment for a house

8: Can you solve this anagram to discover the political cameo in this season?

THEM BALDING ARIEL

9: Where do Lorelai and Rory go to belatedly celebrate Rory's 21st birthday now that they are reconciled?
   a: Las Vegas
   b: Biloxi
   c: Reno
   d: Atlantic City

10: When Lorelai tells Logan that she blames him for Rory's arrest, dropping out of Yale and moving out, how long does she say Rory didn't speak to her for?
   a: Three months and two weeks
   b: Four months, two weeks and five days
   c: Five months, three weeks and sixteen days
   d: Six months

LIFE'S SHORT, QUIZ HARD.

11: How does Lorelai find out about April?
    a: April tells Lorelai that her father owns the diner
    b: Luke tells her over dinner
    c: Rory meets April at the diner
    d: Taylor tells her after monitoring the diner

12: Rory and Logan plan a trip to Asia for their summer, but what does Logan's father expect him to do instead?
    a: Spend the summer at the family house in Maine
    b: Work in London for a year
    c: Get a journalism fellowship
    d: Intern at one of the family newspapers

13: What does Zach need to do in order to gain Mrs Kim's blessing to marry Lane?
    a: Write a hit song
    b: Get baptised
    c: Leave the band
    d: Join the church choir

14: Although Rory is angry with Logan for cheating, what makes her realise she still loves him?
    a: She kisses Marty
    b: She kisses Dean
    c: She kisses Jess
    d: He calls her and says sorry

SEASON 6

15: When Emily tells Lorelai she wants to buy her and Luke a house, what does Lorelai finally tell her?
   a: She wants to move out of Stars Hollow
   b: The wedding is not going to happen
   c: Luke doesn't want to move in with her
   d: April doesn't want them to get married

16: In the season finale, Lorelai finally tells Luke she is tired of waiting and asks him to elope with her straight away. When he says no, what does she do?
   a: She goes to stay at the Inn
   b: She slaps him
   c: She cries and goes home
   d: She goes to Christopher's house

Rory and Logan

Everyone needs a university boyfriend, someone interesting (and very rich) you can have fun with. Then, when it becomes clear life is taking you in different directions, you can amicably split up. Or, you can propose. For heaven's sake, Logan . . .

1: What is Logan's nickname for Rory?

2: Mitchum Huntzberger is Logan's father and a powerful man in a field Rory is interested in. Which businesses does he own?

LIFE'S SHORT, QUIZ HARD.

3: What prank does Rory get her grandfather to play on Logan to get him back for interrupting her class with an embarrassing stunt?
    a: Richard pretends he has complained to the Dean about Logan
    b: Richard pretends Logan and Rory are having an arranged wedding
    c: Richard pretends Lorelai is furious with Logan
    d: Richard pretends Mitchum has disinherited Logan

4: What reason does Logan give for not asking Rory out?
    a: He is not boyfriend material
    b: He already has a girlfriend
    c: They are too different
    d: She is in the year below him

5: When Logan's family is very disapproving of Rory over dinner when they first meet, how does she react?
    a: She is outraged
    b: She breaks up with him on the spot
    c: She cries
    d: She storms out

RORY AND LOGAN

6: What does Logan steal from Emily at his first Friday Night Dinner?
    a: A carriage clock
    b: An antique sewing box
    c: A silver hairbrush
    d: A bottle of port

7: Emily is delighted by the bag that Logan buys Rory. Which bag is it?

8: Logan's sister has four bridesmaids at her wedding. Rory is shocked to find out that how many of them have been involved with Logan?

9: Why did Logan give Rory a rocket as a present when he went to London?

10: Why is Logan angry with Rory's article on his startup launch party?
    a: It spells the startup's name wrong
    b: It is factually incorrect
    c: It is mean and judgemental
    d: She didn't have permission to write it

11: How does Logan travel to the hospital to be with Rory after her grandfather's heart attack?

Yale

Though primarily known for being a type of key in the UK, Yale is actually also an elite university in the US. Famously part of the Ivy League, which disappointingly isn't a superhero thing but just means one of the big, posh universities, it represents a dream coming true for Rory and Lorelai. It is also part of the widening world that Rory finds herself part of as the show progresses.

1: Which home comfort did Rory bring to Yale?
   a: Her childhood cuddly toy
   b: Her own mattress
   c: A framed photo of Lorelai
   d: Her favourite cushion

LIFE'S SHORT, QUIZ HARD.

2: How was Rory's name written on her ID?
    a: Roni
    b: Rory
    c: Lorelai
    d: Rori

3: What does Rory do when Lorelai leaves her on her first day at Yale?

4: What is Marty's nickname?

5: How many years have Emily and Richard attended the Harvard–Yale game?
    a: 30
    b: 32
    c: 34
    d: 36

6: What mistake does Lorelai make at the Harvard–Yale game?
    a: She wears blue
    b: She wears orange
    c: She wears red
    d: She wears green

7: What is Rory's job in her first year at Yale?

8: How does Logan know Marty?

YALE

9: Where does Rory live in the second year at Yale?
   a: Branford College
   b: Saybrook College
   c: Davenport College
   d: Pierson College

10: When Rory goes back to Yale after dropping out, who does she live with?

11: Once Christopher starts paying for Yale, what do Rory's grandparents want to do with the money they would have spent on her tuition?

12: What is Rory's major?

Paris Geller

Paris is a source of conflict for Rory to begin with, as two high-achievers take up the same space, but they eventually come to an understanding that deepens into friendship. Intense, ambitious and relentlessly honest, she is both complex and relatable as a character.

1: Paris and Rory win a school debate competition together. What is the subject of the debate?
   a: Assisted suicide
   b: Animal testing
   c: Capital punishment
   d: The legalisation of cannabis

LIFE'S SHORT, QUIZ HARD.

2: When Dean becomes angry to find Jess at Rory's house when Lorelai is away for the night, what does Paris say to calm the situation?
    a: That Dean has no right to be so possessive
    b: That she likes Jess and Rory asked him round to set them up
    c: That Jess was joining them for a book club discussion
    d: That Lorelai asked Jess to deliver some food for their study session

3: Why does Paris ask Rory to run as her student vice-president?
    a: Headmaster Charleston likes Rory the best
    b: Paris needs a female vice-president
    c: Rory is a great public speaker
    d: Rory is more likeable

4: Can you solve this anagram to reveal where Paris met Jamie, a student from Princeton she dates in Season 3?

GIANT SHOWN

PARIS GELLER

5: Why did Paris record her Harvard interview?
   a: To listen back and learn from her mistakes
   b: To archive and donate to the university on her demise
   c: To share with future applicants
   d: To use in case of a potential appeal

6: We find out Paris's middle name at the Chilton graduation. What is it?
   a: Eustace
   b: Clancey
   c: Blake
   d: Gladwyn

7: Who accompanies Paris to Yale?

8: Why was Paris's relationship with Asher Fleming controversial?

9: Who does Paris end up getting together with at a speed-dating night?

10: Which martial art is Paris trained in?

LIFE'S SHORT, QUIZ HARD.

11: Why does Paris throw out Rory's things from her apartment, which leads to her moving in with Logan?
    a: Rory got the highest marks in their finals
    b: Rory kissed Doyle
    c: Rory was elected editor of the *Yale Daily News*
    d: Rory was awarded a fellowship they both wanted

12: How many law and medical school acceptances does Paris receive?
    a: 4
    b: 6
    c: 8
    d: 10

Sookie St. James

A creative, if sporadically clumsy, chef at the Independence Inn, Sookie is Lorelai's best friend, and their relationship is one of the emotional hearts of the show.

1: Sookie and Jackson's first date is a double date. Who are the other couple?
    a: Lorelai and Luke
    b: Lorelai and Jackson's brother Beau
    c: Lorelai and Max
    d: Lorelai and Jackson's cousin Rune

2: What does Sookie name the cake that she made for Lorelai and Max's wedding?
    a: Clyde
    b: Fred
    c: Bruno
    d: Dylan

LIFE'S SHORT, QUIZ HARD.

3: Can you solve this anagram to discover the name of the actor who plays Jackson's brother, Beau?

MR COFFIN KANE

4: Who wins Sookie's basket in the basket auction?
   a: Jackson
   b: Kirk
   c: Taylor
   d: Lorelai

5: When Sookie meets Lorelai's grandmother, she is really impressed with Sookie's cooking but also notices something about her uniform. What is wrong?
   a: There is a big burn down the front
   b: One arm has been torn off
   c: There is a large cut at the back
   d: The bottom has been ripped off

6: Why is Sookie shocked at the number of children Jackson wants to have?
   a: He wants two children in two years
   b: He wants three children in three years
   c: He wants four children in four years
   d: He doesn't want children

7. Why does Sookie get drunk when Jackson cooks the turkey on Thanksgiving?

SOOKIE ST. JAMES

8. Why is Sookie angry at Norman Mailer's order at the Dragonfly Inn restaurant?

9. Which singer would eat appetizers, main course and two or three desserts when Sookie was cooking at the Independence Inn?
    a: Billy Joel
    b: Sting
    c: Bono
    d: Elton John

10: When does Sookie's baby pager finally go off to let Lorelai know she has gone into labour?
    a: During the Stars Hollow Battle reenactment
    b: During the Festival of Living Pictures
    c: At Friday Night Dinner
    d: At Christmas

11: What are the names of Sookie and Jackson's children?

Season 7

As any gymnast knows, sticking the landing is all-important. So, luckily, Season 7, first broadcast on 26 September 2006, was universally greeted as the perfect way to end the show. Only kidding. Things got real. The creator, Amy Sherman-Palladino, left the show over a variety of creative and contractual differences, and the job of landing the plane was given to a new crew. This led to a slower pace of dialogue and some character resolutions that weren't always beloved by fans.

SEASON 7

1: Luke turns up at Lorelai's in the premiere episode packed and ready to elope. What does Lorelai tell him?
   a: She is leaving town
   b: He's missed his chance
   c: She slept with Christopher
   d: She is too busy to go now

2: Lane returns from her honeymoon with Zach, and he thinks she is avoiding him. What is the real reason she is acting strangely?
   a: She wants an annulment
   b: She is pregnant
   c: She wants to go back on holiday
   d: She misses her mother

3: How does Emily find out that Christopher and Lorelai are dating again?
   a: They come to pick her up from the police station together
   b: Lorelai brings Christopher to Friday Night Dinner as a surprise
   c: They gatecrash one of her Daughters of the American Revolution (DAR) events together
   d: Rory calls her because she knows she will be overjoyed

LIFE'S SHORT, QUIZ HARD.

4: Lorelai and Christopher attend Yale Parents Weekend together. Who do they take out for lunch?
    a: Rory and Paris
    b: The whole of the *Yale Daily News* staff
    c: Rory and Logan
    d: Rory, Emily and Richard

5: When Lorelai and Christopher tell Rory they got married in Paris, Christopher explains that the ceremony was in French, so there is a chance that what happened instead?
    a: They got a very expensive dog licence
    b: They became French citizens
    c: They graduated from Sciences Po
    d: He changed his name

6: Lorelai spends a lot of time stressing about writing Luke's character reference. Why does he need one?
    a: He is on bail for punching Christopher
    b: He wants to buy another location for the diner
    c: He is going to court to get shared custody of April
    d: He wants to run for town selectman

SEASON 7

7: What is Paris's 'Operation Finish Line'?
   a: Her plan to get her parents back together
   b: The working title of her memoir
   c: Her plan to get Doyle to propose
   d: Everything she and Rory need to do to get a job, fellowship or into grad school

8: Can you solve this anagram to discover the actor who cameoed as a Yale friend in this season?

TERRY TRINKETS

9: Why does Sookie not realise she is pregnant for the third time?
   a: She thinks Jackson got a vasectomy
   b: She feels completely fine
   c: Her food still tastes great
   d: She is in a good mood all the time

10: What happens when Rory attends her grandfather's class at Yale?
   a: She falls asleep because it's so boring
   b: He criticises her in front of the class
   c: Paris has an argument with him about Marx
   d: He has a heart attack

LIFE'S SHORT, QUIZ HARD.

11: How does Lane get to her baby shower?
   a: Rory and Lorelai carry her
   b: On a segway
   c: Wheeled in her bed
   d: Kirk drives her

12: Where do Lorelai and Luke have a heart-to-heart about the breakdown of their relationship?
   a: In the Hale Bale Maze
   b: In the diner
   c: At the Black, White and Read Theatre
   d: At the Summer Festival

13: Where does Logan propose to Rory?

14: After a few rejections, Rory gets a job reporting the campaign trail for which Democratic candidate?
   a: Hillary Clinton
   b: Barack Obama
   c: John Edwards
   d: Joe Biden

15: Where do Luke and Lorelai finally kiss and make up?
   a: In the diner
   b: At Rory's going-away party
   c: At the Summer Festival
   d: Under the gazebo in the town square

SEASON 7

16: What is the setting of the last scene of the whole series?
    a: The town meeting
    b: Friday Night Dinner
    c: Luke's Diner
    d: The living room at Lorelai's house

Random Dates

Although Lorelai and Rory both have three serious relationships over the course of the series, we see a couple of other guys try their chances with a Gilmore Girl but who aren't able to go the distance.

1: Who does Rory kiss just after her breakup with Dean at Madeline's party?

2: Where does Lorelai meet Paul, who turns out to be much younger than she initially thought?
   a: At the diner
   b: In her business class
   c: At Friday Night Dinner
   d: He is a Chilton dad

LIFE'S SHORT, QUIZ HARD.

3: In Season 3, Lorelai is shocked when a Stars Hollow resident asks her out and she politely turns him down. Who is it?

4: Who is Lorelai dating when she gets involved with Max again?
    a: Alex
    b: Paul
    c: Jason
    d: Christopher

5: In her first weeks at Yale, Rory goes on a terrible date with Trevor. In which class did she meet him?

6. Using a simple alphanumeric substitution cipher in which B=2 and K=11, can you solve the slightly Maddening love interest for Lorelai?

    10 – 15 – 14

    8 – 1 – 13 – 13

7: What childhood nickname does Lorelai use to annoy Jason?

8: After an awkward date in a silent room at the China Garden, where do Jason and Lorelai go to get food on the way back home?

RANDOM DATES

9: Who uncovers Lorelai and Jason's secret romance?
   a: Richard
   b: Emily
   c: A private investigator
   d: Jason's father

10: Rory lets Marty, a Yale friend, down gently since she is not interested. When she sees him again because he is dating one of her friends, what is she surprised by?
   a: He has changed his accent
   b: He acts like he doesn't know her
   c: He is wearing a wig
   d: He is going by a different name

Extra-Curricular

Rory throws herself into a huge range of activities during the course of the show, and these are key to her journey of discovering who she wants to be.

1: Who is Rory's editor at the Chilton student paper?

2: When Rory first starts at Yale, who is the editor of the *Yale Daily News*?

3: Rory writes a critical review for the *Yale Daily News* as one of her first articles. Who confronts her in the dining hall about it?
    a: An actor
    b: An opera singer
    c: A ballerina
    d: A pianist

LIFE'S SHORT, QUIZ HARD.

4: What did Rory have to make as part of her initiation as a new staffer at the *Yale Daily News*?

5: Why does Paris make everyone at the *Yale Daily News* wear hats with numbers on?
    a: So she doesn't need to learn their names
    b: They are hats from their advertisers
    c: She has introduced a uniform for staffers
    d: They lost a bet

6: All of the *Yale Daily News* staff quit under Paris in protest. What was the first sign that something was wrong?
    a: The newspaper went to press with a missing opinion column
    b: The newspaper went to press without a headline
    c: The newspaper didn't make it to press for the first time in its history
    d: The newspaper went to press with a blank photo in the sports page

7: Who becomes editor of the *Yale Daily News* after Paris's breakdown?

8: Why does Rory call a *Wall Street Journal* journalist to clarify their interview with Mitchum Huntzberger?

EXTRA-CURRICULAR

9: Mitchum offers Rory a job with one of his newspapers if she does what?
   a: Leaves Logan
   b: Helps keep Logan on the right career path
   c: Puts in a good word for Mitchum with Richard
   d: Asks Emily to let Mitchum's wife into the DAR

10: Rory gets rejected from the Reston Fellowship, her dream fellowship. Which newspaper is it with?

11: What type of animal mask do the Life and Death Brigade wear when Rory first encounters them?

12: What are the conditions Logan gives to Rory in order to attend and report on the 108th assembly of the Life and Death Brigade?
   a: She must leave the event at sunset
   b: No photos, names or defining physical characteristics
   c: He has veto on the final article
   d: She must use a pseudonym

13: What is the motto of the Life and Death Brigade?

14: What work does Rory do for the DAR when she drops out of Yale?

LIFE'S SHORT, QUIZ HARD.

15: Where is Logan when he gets injured doing a Life and Death Brigade stunt?

Luke Danes

Everyone needs a Luke. In his backwards baseball cap and flannel shirt, his tough exterior belies a loyal and loving core, and his relationship with Lorelai is one of the most important of the show. Though he might complain about it constantly, he's also a central part of the Stars Hollow community.

1: Who did Luke get married to and divorced from?

2: What are Lorelai and Kirk talking about while Luke is trying to sign his divorce papers?
    a: Their love of *I Dream of Jeannie*
    b: Their love of *Bewitched*
    c: Their love of *The Munsters*
    d: Their love of *Charmed*

LIFE'S SHORT, QUIZ HARD.

3: Which three of the following characters has Luke had a physical altercation with?
   a: Dean
   b: Jess
   c: Kirk
   d: Taylor
   e: Christopher
   f: TJ

4: Why does Luke volunteer to help with Old Man Twickham's house?

5: Why is 30 November Luke's 'dark day'?

6: What does Luke give Rory for her 21st birthday?
   a: A pearl necklace
   b: A pearl bracelet
   c: A ruby necklace
   d: A ruby bracelet

7: What is the name of April's mother?

8: How long does Luke keep the fact that April is his daughter secret from Lorelai?
   a: 1 month
   b: 2 months
   c: 3 months
   d: 4 months

LUKE DANES

9: Which nickname do April's friends give Luke?
   a: Dumbledore
   b: Hagrid
   c: Harry
   d: Weasley

10: Why is April's mother angry about the birthday party that Luke threw for April?
   a: Lorelai planned it
   b: Luke forgot the cake
   c: She wasn't invited
   d: April said she didn't want a party

11: What does Luke do when he finds out that Lorelai slept with Christopher after he refused to elope with her?
   a: Bans Christopher from the diner
   b: Calls Christopher to shout at him
   c: Punches Christopher in the face
   d: Calls Nicole

12: Luke dates Coach Bennett in Season 7. What sport does she coach?
   a: Swimming
   b: Lacrosse
   c: Football
   d: Hockey

LIFE'S SHORT, QUIZ HARD.

13: Why does Anna tell Luke that she and April are going to move to New Mexico?

Friday Night Dinners

Which of the following were five acceptable reasons for Rory skipping Friday Night Dinner:
- a: Lorelai's birthday
- b: Rory and Dean's anniversary
- c: Lane's graduation
- d: Telling Dean about the car accident with Jess
- e: Sookie going into labour
- f: Having a cold
- g: Logan leaving for London
- h: Rory meeting Sherry
- i: Last-minute finals cramming
- j: Sherry going into labour

Christopher Hayden

Care-free in the way only someone whose wealthy parents have paid for his motorbike can be, Christopher drifts in and out of Lorelai and Rory's lives in the early seasons. By the end of the show, he has built a relationship with Rory and supports her at Yale with his own inheritance.

1: Where is Christopher working at the start of the series?
    a: A law firm
    b: An insurance firm
    c: An internet startup
    d: A hospital

LIFE'S SHORT, QUIZ HARD.

2: What was Christopher attempting to buy Rory when his card was declined?
    a: Lunch
    b: An *Oxford English Dictionary*
    c: A car
    d: A lamp

3: What are the names of Christopher's parents?

4: Why does Sherry leave Christopher?

5: With apologies to sticklers for umlauts, can you solve this anagram to discover the actress who played Christopher's girlfriend in Season 2 and 3?

    MANMADE CHICK

6: Why did Christopher turn up out of the blue to visit Rory at Yale in her second year?
    a: He wanted to redecorate her suite for her birthday
    b: To ask her to help him get Lorelai back
    c: He was there at an alumni event
    d: His father was sick and it made him want to improve his relationship with her

CHRISTOPHER HAYDEN

7: Who does Christopher inherit a large amount of money from?
    a: His mother
    b: His father
    c: His grandmother
    d: His grandfather

8: What trendy phone does Christopher buy Rory?
    a: A Motorola Razr
    b: A BlackBerry
    c: A Sidekick
    d: A Palm Pilot

9: How does Sherry apologise to Christopher for leaving Gigi and ask to be involved in her life again?
    a: In person
    b: By letter
    c: By email
    d: By phone

A Year in the Life

Nine years and six months after the final episode of Season 7 was broadcast, on 25 November 2016 the first episode of *Gilmore girls: A Year in the Life* dropped on Netflix. Helmed by Amy Sherman-Palladino, it was universally greeted as the perfect . . . Only kidding. Like any of life's most important relationships, it can be hard to go back years later. Then again, it's better to have new *Gilmore girls* than no *Gilmore girls*. The return to Stars Hollow shows us our favourite characters ten years on and ends on a surprise cliffhanger, leaving us to wonder what happens next for Rory and Lorelai.

A Year in the Life 'Winter'

1: Rory comes to Stars Hollow on a flying one-day visit from which city?

LIFE'S SHORT, QUIZ HARD.

2: What does Rory bring Lorelai as a present?
   a: Prince George-branded iced-tea spoons
   b: Princess Charlotte-branded iced-tea spoons
   c: Prince William-branded iced-tea spoons
   d: Prince Harry-branded iced-tea spoons

3: Emily is shocked that Rory has no fixed address. Where was the apartment she just gave up?
   a: Brooklyn
   b: Long Island
   c: Manhattan
   d: Queens

4: Rory has a very forgettable boyfriend, called Paul. How long have they been together?
   a: 6 months
   b: 1 year
   c: 2 years
   d: 3 years

5: Lorelai wakes up to find Rory doing what type of dancing in the kitchen?

A YEAR IN THE LIFE

6: Taylor reveals that Luke doesn't want to give anyone the Wi-Fi password for the diner and just makes them up on the spot. Which two does he give out this episode?
   a: Dinerluke
   b: DINERDANES321
   c: StrongCoffee
   d: GOAWAYTAYLOR*

7: What has Luke printed on the back of the diner menu?

8: Which food truck chef does Lorelai throw out of the Dragonfly Inn kitchen, even though they were meant to do a pop-up there for two weeks?
   a: David Chang
   b: Anthony Bourdain
   c: Roy Choi
   d: Ina Garten

9: How long has Sookie been away?

10: Kirk provides a driving service where he can also sing to his passengers any song from which band's catalogue?
   a: Backstreet Boys
   b: The Beach Boys
   c: Billy Joel
   d: The Carpenters

LIFE'S SHORT, QUIZ HARD.

11: How old is Rory?
    a: 31
    b: 32
    c: 33
    d: 34

12: Sadly, Richard died four months earlier. Why are Rory and Lorelai shocked by the painting Emily has had made of him?

13: Which old boyfriend of Lorelai's comes to Richard's funeral?

14: Can you solve this anagram to discover the cult TV show that Ray Wise, who plays Jack Smith, is the third actor to appear from in *Gilmore girls*?

KANT WIPES

15: How long have Emily and Lorelai been out of contact for?
    a: 2 months
    b: 4 months
    c: 6 months
    d: 8 months

16: Lorelai and Luke explore surrogacy. Who is the doctor they visit for a consultation?

A YEAR IN THE LIFE

17: Rory stays with Logan in London. What saying encapsulates their relationship status?
   a: 'What happens in Vegas, stays in Vegas'
   b: 'Absence makes the heart grow fonder'
   c: 'While the cat's away, the mice will play'
   d: 'If you love someone, let them go'

18: Paris and Doyle are going through a divorce. What is Doyle's job now?

19: How long were Emily and Richard married for?
   a: 40 years
   b: 50 years
   c: 55 years
   d: 60 years

20: For the first time, Emily takes Lorelai's advice and does what?
   a: Goes on a solo holiday
   b: Buys a motorbike
   c: Sees a therapist
   d: Fires the household staff

A Year in the Life, 'Spring'

1: Which character do we meet for the first time, who was mentioned but never appeared in seven seasons?

LIFE'S SHORT, QUIZ HARD.

2: At the Stars Hollow International food festival, how many countries show up out of a possible 195?

3: At a town meeting, Taylor wants to hold a Stars Hollow Gay Pride Parade in 2016, as the year coincides with which event?
　　a: Liza Minnelli's 60th birthday
　　b: Liza Minnelli's 70th birthday
　　c: Barbra Streisand's 60th birthday
　　d: Barbra Streisand's 70th birthday

4: Which two celebrities are staying at a nearby town?
　　a: Matthew McConaughey
　　b: Jessica Chastain
　　c: Tom Cruise
　　d: Nicole Kidman

5: How many rooms are at the Dragonfly Inn?
　　a: 5
　　b: 10
　　c: 15
　　d: 20

6: Where does Rory tell her mother she is staying in London (instead of Logan's)?

A YEAR IN THE LIFE

7: Where is Rory and Logan's traditional farewell meal in London?
   a: Soho House
   b: The Ritz
   c: The Ivy
   d: The Wolseley

8: What is the name of Logan's fiancée?

9: Can you solve this anagram to reveal which David Lynch film is being shown at the Black, White and Read Movie Theatre?

HEARSE DARE

10: Why didn't Emily get Lorelai's message that she was coming to dinner?
   a: She accidentally deleted it before reading it
   b: She left her phone at the club
   c: The maid didn't pass the message on
   d: She doesn't do email

11: Why does Rory stay the night at her grandmother's house?

12: Why does Emily want to meet with Luke on his own?

LIFE'S SHORT, QUIZ HARD.

13: How much did Paris donate to the Chilton capital improvement plan?
 a: $1,000
 b: $10,000
 c: $100,000
 d: $1,000,000

14: What does Emily call Lorelai and Luke in therapy?
 a: Roommates with benefits
 b: Friends with benefits
 c: Romantic roomies
 d: Live-in lovers

15: Paris freaks out when she sees who at the Chilton alumni event?

16: What is in Paris's briefcase?

17: Rory offers to write a spec article for *GQ* on which topic?

18: What pastry does Lorelai manage to procure?
 a: A cruffin
 b: A cronut
 c: A cro-dough-cake
 d: Crookie-dough

A YEAR IN THE LIFE

19: Rory has her first one-night stand with a guy wearing which *Star Wars* costume?
   a: An Ewok
   b: A stormtrooper
   c: Darth Vader
   d: A Wookie

20: How many phones does Rory have?
   a: 1
   b: 2
   c: 3
   d: 4

A Year in the Life, 'Summer'

1: Now a student at MIT, how old is April?
   a: 20
   b: 21
   c: 22
   d: 23

2: Why is Rory upset when she calls Logan about her forthcoming visit to London?

3: Who are the 30-Something Gang?

LIFE'S SHORT, QUIZ HARD.

4: The *Stars Hollow Gazette* is shutting down after how many years of operation?
 a: 79
 b: 89
 c: 99
 d: 109

5: What unusual skill does the leading lady need for the Stars Hollow musical?
 a: Fire eating
 b: Juggling
 c: Walking on her hands
 d: Whittling

6: What job does Rory volunteer to do for free and starts immediately?

7: Who plays the live music at the Secret Bar?

8: What does the Five-O warning shout mean at the Secret Bar?
 a: Kirk has spilt something
 b: Taylor is on his way
 c: Miss Patty is drunk
 d: Luke is angry

A YEAR IN THE LIFE

9: What does Rory remove from the front page of the *Gazette*?
 a: The poem
 b: The opinion column
 c: The adverts
 d: The editor photo

10: Where is Michel considering moving to?
 a: The W Hotel in San Francisco
 b: The W Hotel in New Orleans
 c: The W Hotel in Las Vegas
 d: The W Hotel in New York

11: Who was the previous editor at the *Stars Hollow Gazette*?

12: Which director do the 30-Something Gang love?
 a: David Lynch
 b: Paul Thomas Anderson
 c: Christopher Nolan
 d: Wes Anderson

LIFE'S SHORT, QUIZ HARD.

13: Can you solve this riddle to discover the director that Doyle is currently working for?

My first is in moronically but not in ironically
My second is in ringleader but not in dangler
My third is in mortification but not in informant
My fourth is in scratchily but not in sarcastically
My fifth is in ingrain but not in rigging
My sixth is in admirer but not in midair
My seventh is in repel but not in peeper
My first is in obtain but not in notation
My second is in blamelessness but not in ensemble
My third is in tenacity but not in ancient

14: Carole King (as the character Sophie) plays one of her own songs, which is turned down for the musical. Which one?
  a: 'I Feel the Earth Move'
  b: 'You've Got a Friend'
  c: 'Where You Lead, I Will Follow'
  d: 'Fire and Rain'

15: Who did Lorelai play in her one musical role?
  a: Cosette in *Les Misérables*
  b: Golde in *Fiddler on the Roof*
  c: Lucy in *You're a Good Man, Charlie Brown*
  d: Eva Perón in *Evita*

A YEAR IN THE LIFE

16: Emily gets a new gravestone for Richard as the other ones had errors. What number is this one?
   a: The third
   b: The fourth
   c: The fifth
   d: The sixth

17: What is wrong with this gravestone?

18: Jess comes to visit Rory at the *Gazette* offices. What does he tell Rory to write a book about?

19: Why doesn't Lorelai want Rory to write her book?

20: After arguments with Rory and Luke, what does Lorelai leave to do?
   a: Fly to Jamaica inspired by *How Stella Got Her Groove Back*
   b: Tour Italy following *Eat, Pray, Love*
   c: Live in Greece like *Mamma Mia!*
   d: Hike the Pacific West Trail from *Wild*

A Year in the Life, 'Fall'

1: How do the women hiking the Pacific West Trail divide themselves?

LIFE'S SHORT, QUIZ HARD.

2: Rory sees Kirk's pig running down the street with a sign pinned to it. What does it say?
    a: 'Hello Rory!'
    b: 'Let the wild rumpus start'
    c: 'Kick up a rumpus'
    d: 'Gone to market'

3: What does Luke accidentally tell a customer in the diner due to distraction over Lorelai being away?

4: Logan turns up in Stars Hollow with Finn, Colin and Robert from the Life and Death Brigade. They end up in a tango club, but what does Colin do when he doesn't like the music at the club?

5: Logan tries to give Rory a key so that she has a place to write her book. Where does he suggest?
    a: His family house in Maine
    b: His apartment in London
    c: His holiday house in Italy
    d: His empty office in New York

6: Why doesn't the Park Ranger allow Lorelai on the trail?

7: Where is the perfect place Rory has found to write her book?

A YEAR IN THE LIFE

8: Lorelai comes back with the realisation that she wants to get married to Luke. What day do they set the wedding for?
   a: Lorelai's birthday
   b: Halloween
   c: Harvest Festival
   d: Their anniversary

9: Why does Emily say that being the fourth wife to a wealthy man is a good position to be in?
   a: You are likely to outlive him
   b: He might be too exhausted to look for wife number five
   c: He has learnt from his previous mistakes
   d: He won't want children

10: Can you solve this anagram to reveal the one person Luke wants to invite to his wedding?

ELFISH UNDERTAKER

11: Emily sells the Gilmore mansion and buys a house in Nantucket. It was called the Clam Shack. What does she change it to?
   a: Richard's Place
   b: The Beach House
   c: Seaside Cottage
   d: The Sandcastle

LIFE'S SHORT, QUIZ HARD.

12: What does Lorelai want to use Luke's franchise money for?

13: What is Emily's condition for Lorelai to use Luke's franchise money?

14: When Sookie arrives after two years away, what has she filled the Dragonfly Inn kitchen with?
    a: Wedding cakes
    b: New cookware
    c: Recipe books
    d: Flowers

15: Why did Lorelai take Sookie to the hospital the first day they met?

16: When Rory bumps into Dean at Doose's, what does she ask him?
    a: If he misses her
    b: If he regrets how it ended between them
    c: If he minds being in her book
    d: How often he is in Stars Hollow

17: Lorelai doesn't read the three chapters Rory gives her of the book and says she will read it when it's finished. What is her one note about the title, 'The Gilmore girls'?

A YEAR IN THE LIFE

18: Luke and Lorelai decide to get married the night before the wedding to ease the stress of the next day. What song is playing while they get married?
   a: Richard's favourite song
   b: Their favourite song
   c: The song they first danced to
   d: The song they first kissed to

19: How do Rory and Paul finally break up?

20: What are the last words of the whole series?

Answers

Gilmore Haste, Less Speed

1.
c: Lorelai and Rory must attend dinner at their house every Friday

2.
a: 16.

3.
b: 15. She has her 16th birthday during the first season of the series

4.
c: Lorelai. Lorelai named her daughter after herself, and she is nicknamed Rory.

LIFE'S SHORT, QUIZ HARD.

5.
d: Christopher Hayden, Lorelai's high school boyfriend who leaves her to raise Rory alone

6.
a: Stars Hollow

7.
b: Connecticut

8.
c: At the Independence Inn, working as a maid

9.
c: Christmas, Thanksgiving and Easter

10.
c: Lane Kim

11.
b: She is a chef

12.
d: To own her own inn

13.
a: Luke Danes

14.
b: Harvard

ANSWERS

15.
c: 7

16.
b: 2000

17.
b: 2007

18.
b: 2016, *Gilmore girls: A Year in the Life*

19.
a: There were four episodes, each named after one of the four seasons: 'Spring', 'Summer', 'Autumn' and 'Winter'

20.
b: Amy Sherman-Palladino

Season 1

1.
b: Stars Hollow High (Season 1, Episode 1)

2.
d: D (Season 1, Episode 4)

3.
a: Episode 1, 'Pilot'

LIFE'S SHORT, QUIZ HARD.

4.
a: At her grandparents', on Friday night
and
c: At her house in Stars Hollow, on Saturday night (Season 1, Episode 6)

5.
d: Mrs Kim, Lane's mother (Season 1, Episode 7)

6.
b: A bake sale at Chilton (Season 1, Episode 5)

7.
c: Frozen pizza (Season 1, Episode 8)

8.
c: Tristan (Season 1, Episode 9)

9.
Jane Lynch (Season 1, Episode 10)

10.
b: Luke (Season 1, Episode 10)

11.
a: Business

12.
a: 0; this is his first time

ANSWERS

13.

c: Dean was upset that he told Rory 'I love you' and she didn't feel ready to say it back (Season 1, Episode 16)

14.

d: A tool shed at the Independence Inn (Season 1, Episode 19)

15.

b: Her grandparents' house (Season 1, Episode 20)

16.

c: Not to wait too long to tell Lorelai how he feels (Season 1, Episode 21)

Lorelai and Max

1.
English

2.
Coffee (Season 1, Episode 5)

3.
b: *Swann's Way* by Proust (Season 1, Episode 11)

4.
Paris (Season 1, Episode 11)

LIFE'S SHORT, QUIZ HARD.

5.
c: That she slept with Rory's dad on her parents' balcony (Episode 21)

6.
c: 1,000 yellow daisies, delivered by Kirk to the Inn (Season 1, Episode 21)

7.
University of Toronto

8.
a: An ice-cream maker (Season 2, Episode 9)

9.
California

Home Sweet Home
1.
A: Doose's

2.
b: 9,973 (Season 1, Episode 2)

3.
The antiques store

ANSWERS

4.
Town meetings. The first town meeting was in Season 1, Episode 8.

5.
Residents could only shop at one store or the other, affecting the economy of the town (Season 5, Episode 3)

6.
His house, to be turned into a museum (Season 5, Episode 18)

7.
Traffic lights (Season 2, Episode 2)

8.
Kirk forgot where he put them (Season 4, Episode 18)

9.
c: A woman's role is included for the first time, once it comes to light that a Stars Hollow resident tempted a soldier to stay the night with her and saved the town (Season 5, Episode 11)

10.
c: A Botox party (Season 5, Episode 15)

LIFE'S SHORT, QUIZ HARD.

Emily Gilmore

1.
a: Louis Vuitton (Season 5, Episode 11)

2.
b: The female Pol Pot (Season 5, Episode 18)

3.
d: That he is not allowed to die before her (Season 1, Episode 10)

4.
c: Sookie invites her to the surprise engagement party (Season 2, Episode 1)

5.
d: Luke's Diner (Season 5, Episode 7)

6.
b: She exclaimed that Rory was not fried chicken and that the house wasn't a drive-thru (Season 1, Episode 9)

7.
a: She bursts into tears (Season 5, Episode 9)

8.
She thinks he needs to get back together with Lorelai (Season 5, Episode 13 – the 100th episode of the series!)

ANSWERS

9.
Guilt and Chanel No. 5 (Season 4, Episode 3)

10.
Europe (Season 5, Episode 1)

11.
At Lorelai's house (Season 5, Episode 13)

12.
a: She tries to buy a plane (Season 6, Episode 9)

13.
d: A cocktail waitress (Season 6, Episode 13)

I Like Big Books and I Cannot Lie

1.
Rory (Season 1, Episode 5)

2.
Rory (Season 1, Episode 12)

3.
Jess (Season 3, Episode 2)

4.
Jess (Season 2, Episode 21)

LIFE'S SHORT, QUIZ HARD.

5.
Jess (Season 3, Episode 5)

6.
Jess (Season 3, Episode 13)

7.
Jess (Season 3, Episode 20)

8.
Rory (Season 4, Episode 3)

9.
Rory (Season 4, Episode 4)

10.
Rory (Season 5, Episode 15)

Season 2

1.
a: Christopher (Season 2, Episode 2)

2.
c: A chuppah (Season 2, Episode 3)

3.
b: Harvard (Season 2, Episode 4)

ANSWERS

4.

d: A garden gnome, called Pierpont (Season 2, Episode 5)

5.

b: Christopher (Season 2, Episode 6)

6.

a: Paris. Tristan was originally meant to play the part but was sent to military school instead (Season 2, Episode 9)

7.

d: Emily co-signs a loan from the bank (Season 2, Episode 11)

8.

Carole King, owner of the music shop (Season 2, Episode 20)

9.

b: Jess (Season 2, Episode 13)

10.

c: Sherry (Season 2, Episode 14)

11.

d: In a car accident with Jess (Season 2, Episode 19)

12.

c: That he left without saying goodbye (Season 2, Episode 21)

LIFE'S SHORT, QUIZ HARD.

13.
a: Her mother's graduation (Season 2, Episode 21)

14.
b: She has argued with Luke over Jess (Season 2, Episode 21)

15.
c: Sookie's wedding (Season 2, Episode 22)

16.
a: His girlfriend calls and says she is pregnant (Season 2, Episode 22)

Rory and Dean

1.
d: Chicago (Season 1, Episode 1)

2.
A bracelet (Season 1, Episode 6)

3.
a: 'Thank you' (Season 1, Episode 7)

4.
Miss Patty's Ballet School (Season 1, Episode 9)

5.
Jane Austen (Season 1, Episode 8)

ANSWERS

6.
Three months (Season 1, Episode 16)

7.
That she loves him (Season 1, Episode 21)

8.
She writes him a letter that he reads in front of her (Season 2, Episode 20)

9.
Jess (Season 4, Episode 21)

10.
c: Warning Luke about how hard it is to date a Gilmore Girl (Season 5, Episode 18)

Luke's Diner

1.
c: 'No cell phones'

2.
A hardware store (Season 1, Episode 14)

3.
b: The Hungry Diner (Season 2, Episode 20)

4.
Breakfast (Season 3, Episode 17)

LIFE'S SHORT, QUIZ HARD.

5.
c: He adds more salads – three, in fact (Season 3, Episode 16)

6.
a: They hover right behind them (Season 4, Episode 9)

7.
They hate Brennon (Froggy), the new server (Season 4, Episode 9)

8.
Turkey legs (Season 4, Episode 21)

9.
d: Gummy Worms (Season 5, Episode 16)

10.
Caesar

Richard Gilmore

1.
Yale

2.
His mother – Lorelai's grandmother and Rory's great-grandmother – also known as Trix (Season 1, Episode 3)

ANSWERS

3.
c: Nothing is wrong with it (Season 2, Episode 12)

4.
a: He has retired (Season 2, Episode 10)

5.
On the Yale campus when he was a student (Season 3, Episode 8)

6.
The Whiffenpoofs (Season 3, Episode 8)

7.
The son of his previous employer, Floyd Stiles (Season 4, Episode 3)

8.
d: 1 month (Season 4, Episode 9)

9.
Richard's girlfriend before Emily (Season 4, Episode 9)

10.
c: He crashes his car into hers (Season 5, Episode 12)

11.
Her doll's house (Season 6, Episode 6)

LIFE'S SHORT, QUIZ HARD.

12.
Economics (Season 7, Episode 4)

13.
c: He fell off a horse and suddenly he was radish crazy (according to Emily) (Season 7, Episode 5)

Striking a Chord

1.
c: The Bangles (Season 1, Episode 13)

2.
The Offspring (Season 1, Episode 15)

3.
d: PJ Harvey (Season 1, Episode 21)

4.
b: *Beauty and the Beat* by The Go-Go's (Season 2, Episode 21)

5.
c: Dead Kennedys (Season 3, Episode 3)

6.
b: '99 Luftballons' (Season 3, Episode 13)

7.
d: 'London Calling' (Season 3, Episode 4)

ANSWERS

8.
'The Candy Man' (Season 5, Episode 1)

9.
Yo La Tengo and Sonic Youth (Season 6, Episode 22)

10.
Prince (Season 5, Episode 22)

11.
a: 'Hanging on the Telephone' (Season 6, Episode 3)

12.
Gwen Stefani and Gavin Rossdale, drawing a parallel to Gavin Rossdale finding out he was the father to Daisy Lowe and Luke finding out about April (Season 6, Episode 12)

13.
b: The White Stripes (Season 6, Episode 19)

14.
c: Neil Young (Season 6, Episode 21)

15.
d: 'Living on a Prayer' (Season 7, Episode 6)

16.
'My Heart Will Go On' (Season 7, Episode 14)

LIFE'S SHORT, QUIZ HARD.

17.
'I Will Always Love You' (Season 7, Episode 20)

18.
Zach, Lane, Brian and Gil

Season 3

1.
c: She lived with Luke and was pregnant with twins (Season 3, Episode 1)

2.
a: Hillary Clinton (Season 3, Episode 3)

3.
b: He is looking for a drummer for his band and sees her flyer (Season 3, Episode 3)

4.
d: Rory and Lorelai, using devilled eggs from Sherry's baby shower (Season 3, Episode 6)

5.
b: The 24-hour dance marathon (Season 3, Episode 7)

6.
c: An admissions interview for Rory (Season 3, Episode 8)

ANSWERS

7.
a: She leaves them a note and drives herself to the hospital (Season 3, Episode 13)

8.
Adam Brody featured in Season 3 before leaving the show to join *The OC*

9.
c: Gigi

10.
b: A swan attacked him (Season 3, Episode 14)

11.
c: She cooked terrible-tasting food (Season 3, Episode 16)

12.
c: Harvard
d: Yale
g: Princeton (Season 3, Episode 16)

13.
a: They are engaged (Season 3, Episode 20)

14.
c: She wants her mother to be able to buy the Dragonfly Inn (Season 3, Episode 22)

LIFE'S SHORT, QUIZ HARD.

15.
d: Backpacking around Europe (first planned in Season 3, Episode 13)

16.
b: That she tells him not to get engaged to Nicole (Season 3, Episode 22)

Lorelai and Christopher

1.
A motorcycle (Season 1, Episode 14)

2.
c: A gift basket that includes a real pearl necklace (Season 2, Episode 21)

3.
b: Perfect (Season 3, Episode 13)

4.
d: He needs to fight for Lorelai (Season 5, Episode 12)

5.
a: *Snakes on a Plane* (Season 7, Episode 4)

6.
To take Gigi to see her mother (Season 7, Episode 6)

ANSWERS

7.
He convinces a closed restaurant to open just for them (Season 7, Episode 7)

8.
d: Mrs Hayden – they have got married (Season 7, Episode 7)

9.
Lorelai didn't want to leave Stars Hollow, she wasn't interested in the wedding party and she didn't want to have a baby with him (Season 7, Episode 12)

The Dragonfly and Independence Inn
1.
Mia (Season 2, Episode 8)

2.
Rachel shows Lorelai a photo she took of the Dragonfly Inn (Season 1, Episode 9)

3.
Fran, the owner of the bakery (Season 2, Episode 8) – they manage to get the Inn in Season 3, Episode 20, when she dies

4.
a: Jackson (Season 2, Episode 10)

LIFE'S SHORT, QUIZ HARD.

5.
At home (Season 3, Episode 17)

6.
Luke (Season 4, Episode 15)

7.
d: A Big Red chewing gum wrapper (Season 4, Episode 14)

8.
His dogs (Paw-Paw and Chin-Chin) (Season 4, Episode 22)

9.
a: A motor home (Season 5, Episode 17)

10.
c: American Travel (Season 5, Episode 18)

11.
b: Sores and Boils Alley (Season 6, Episode 6)

Taylor Doose
1.
Jess (Season 2, Episode 8)

2.
A soda shoppe (Season 4, Episode 1)

ANSWERS

3.
c: He has a mismatched toupee (Season 4, Episode 18)

4.
He voted against the relationship (Season 5, Episode 3)

5.
a: Jackson (Season 5, Episode 4)

6.
To show which side of the Luke/Lorelai breakup they are on (Season 5, Episode 14)

7.
b: Kirk (Season 6, Episode 12)

8.
c: Kirk crashes his car into Luke's Diner because the camera flash is so bright (Season 7, Episode 1)

9.
a: A train derailed nearby, spilling pickles and pickle brine, and the pickles have been in the sun for three days (Season 7, Episode 5)

(Gilmore) Girls on Film

1.
b: *Willy Wonka & the Chocolate Factory* (Season 1, Episode 7)

LIFE'S SHORT, QUIZ HARD.

2.
a: *The Rocky Horror Picture Show* (Season 2, Episode 11)

3.
d: *Showgirls* (Season 2, Episode 12)

4.
c: *The Yearling* (Season 2, Episode 19)

5.
d: The *Godfather* trilogy (Season 4, Episode 1)

6.
a: *Casablanca* (Season 4, Episode 5)

7.
b: *A Room with a View* (Season 5, Episode 2)

8.
c: *A Star Is Born* (Season 5, Episode 16)

9.
b: *The Wizard of Oz* (Season 6, Episode 11)

10.
a: *American Gigolo* (Season 6, Episode 19)

11.
d: *Pretty in Pink* (Season 6, Episode 20)

ANSWERS

Season 4

1.
a: Friday Night Dinner at the grandparents' (Season 4, Episode 1)

2.
c: They got married and now they are getting divorced (Season 4, Episode 1)

3.
d: Paris (Season 4, Episode 2)

4.
b: Dean's wedding (Season 4, Episode 4)

5.
a: She flinched last time (Season 4, Episode 7)

6.
c: Richard sees his ex-girlfriend once a year for a secret lunch (for the last 39 years!) (Season 4, Episode 9)

7.
b: She has a big argument with her mother (Season 4, Episode 9)

8.
Max Greenfield – Schmidt from *New Girl* (Season 4, Episode 4)

LIFE'S SHORT, QUIZ HARD.

9.
d: Lane wants to be a drummer and practice with her band (Season 4, Episode 11)

10.
b: 'I love you' (Season 4, Episode 12)

11.
a: She found a letter Trix wrote to Richard telling him not to marry Emily (Season 4, Episode 16)

12.
c: Dean (Season 4, Episode 17)

13.
d: Because she can't be with someone who is suing her family (Season 4, Episode 19)

14.
c: They see her leave the house after Friday Night Dinner and Lorelai then calls round local hotels (Season 4, Episode 19)

15.
d: He loves Lorelai (Season 4, Episode 20)

16.
b: After his sister's wedding, when they have their first dance together ever (Season 4, Episode 21)

ANSWERS

Rory and Jess

1.
A chalk outline of a dead body (Season 2, Episode 8)

2.
The bracelet Dean gave her for her 16th birthday (Season 2, Episode 13)

3.
To get ice-cream as a study break (Season 2, Episode 19)

4.
a: Washington Square Park (Season 2, Episode 21)

5.
Shane (Season 3, Episode 1)

6.
b: Rory will think it's his fault (Season 3, Episode 9)

7.
Sherilyn Fenn – the *Twin Peaks* actress plays both Jimmy's (Jess's dad) girlfriend in Season 3, Episode 19 and Anna Nardini, an ex-girlfriend of Luke in Season 6

8.
Walmart (Season 3, Episode 17)

9.
d: His father, Jimmy (Season 3, Episode 21)

LIFE'S SHORT, QUIZ HARD.

10.
To come away with him to New York (Season 4, Episode 21)

11.
a: She can count on him now (Season 4, Episode 21)

12.
The Subsect (Season 6, Episode 8)

13.
Truncheon Books (Season 6, Episode 18)

Stars Hollow Festivals and Events

1.
Battle of Stars Hollow reenactment – November (Season 1, Episode 8)

2.
Stars Hollow holiday pageant/nativity – December (Season 1, Episode 10)

3.
Festival celebrating the founding of Stars Hollow – January (Season 1, Episode 16)

4.
Poe Festival – March (Season 3, Episode 17)

ANSWERS

5.
First Annual Stars Hollow End of Summer Madness Festival – August (Season 3, Episode 1)

6.
24-hour Dance Marathon – November (Season 3, Episode 7)

7.
Winter Carnival – January (Season 3, Episode 10)

8.
Festival of Living Pictures (Season 4, Episode 7)

9.
Cider Mill Parade (Season 5, Episode 1)

10.
Hay Bale Maze (Season 7, Episode 18)

Lane Kim

1.
c: Sales (Season 2, Episode 18)

2.
Henry (Season 1, Episode 17)

3.
Dean Forester (Season 1, Episode 20)

LIFE'S SHORT, QUIZ HARD.

4.
Thanksgiving (Season 3, Episode 9)

5.
The drums (Season 2, Episode 20)

6.
Hep Alien

7.
a: Purple (Season 3, Episode 4)

8.
Rami Malek (Season 4, Episode 11)

9.
c: No alcohol is served and it's within walking distance of a church (Season 4, Episode 9)

10.
She lives with Zach and Brian (Season 4, Episode 21)

11.
a: Their living room

12.
b: Eternal damnation (Season 5, Episode 22)

ANSWERS

13.
b: 2 – one Buddhist and one Christian (Season 6, Episode 19)

14.
b: In kindergarten (Season 6, Episode 19)

Nobody Puts Rory in the Corner

1.
Britney Spears (Season 1, Episode 1)

2.
a: Hugh Grant (Season 1, Episode 11)

3.
b: Charles Manson (Season 1, Episode 15)

4.
a: Chernobyl
b: The Hindenburg (Season 1, Episode 15)

5.
c: Judy Garland (Season 1, Episode 21)

6.
d: Blue Man Group (Season 1, Episode 21)

7.
a: Ivana Trump (Season 2, Episode 1)

LIFE'S SHORT, QUIZ HARD.

8.
c: Herman Munster (Fred Gwynne) (Season 2, Episode 4)

9.
b: A 'vertical *From Here to Eternity* moment' (Season 2, Episode 13)

10.
c: Woody Allen in *Annie Hall* (Season 2, Episode 21)

11.
b: 'Damon to my Affleck' (Season 2, Episode 22)

12.
c: *Blue Velvet* (Season 3, Episode 7)

13.
d: *West Side Story* (Season 3, Episode 9)

14.
a: Howard Stern (Season 3, Episode 13)

15.
c: Cartman (Season 4, Episode 9)

Season 5

1.
c: She finds a letter in Dean's jacket (given to him by Lorelai while Rory is in Europe) (Season 5, Episode 2)

ANSWERS

2.

a: Walking down into the diner (full of breakfast customers) wearing only his shirt (Season 5, Episode 3)

3.

c: They have the wine and cheese with Richard and the main meal with Emily
(Season 5, Episode 3)

4.

b: Rory and Dean (Season 5, Episode 5)

5.

d: She is in a relationship with Luke now (Season 5, Episode 6)

6.

a: At her grandparents' house – they have thrown her a party to meet eligible men (Season 5, Episode 8)

7.

d: 40th (Season 5, Episode 12)

8.

Norman Mailer (Season 5, Episode 6)

9.

c: They find Logan and Rory kissing and argue about who is responsible for Rory (Season 5, Episode 13)

LIFE'S SHORT, QUIZ HARD.

10.
b: Christopher reveals that Emily wants Lorelai with him instead of Luke (Season 5, Episode 13)

11.
c: He offers her an internship at one of his newspapers, the *Stanford Eagle-Gazette* (Season 5, Episode 19)

12.
a: She is in labour (Season 5, Episode 21)

13.
b: She steals a boat and ends up in jail (Season 5, Episode 21)

14.
a: Organises a band tour of churches over the summer (they have to cut out the swearing) (Season 5, Episode 22)

15.
d: Richard and Emily announce Rory will move into their pool house and take time off from Yale (Season 5, Episode 22)

16.
c: 'What?' (Season 5, Episode 22)

ANSWERS

Lorelai and Luke

1.
c: She accidentally buys her old sweater (donated by Luke) at a rummage sale, and Luke is angry to see her wearing it (Season 1, Episode 13)

2.
a: She was never dressed weather-appropriate (Season 4, Episode 20)

3.
b: Sniffy's Tavern (Season 5, Episode 3)

4.
A horoscope (Season 5, Episode 3)

5.
a: 8 years (Season 5, Episode 3)

6.
Christopher (Season 5, Episode 11)

7.
a: To the cinema, to watch *My Man Godfrey* (Season 5, Episode 14)

8.
They want to wait until Lorelai and Rory have reconciled (Season 6, Episode 4)

LIFE'S SHORT, QUIZ HARD.

9.
c: She thinks it is old and creepy (Season 6, Episode 9)

10.
a: 3rd June (Season 6, Episode 11)

11.
c: April is now in his life

12.
a: At the hospital – April is there with appendicitis (Season 7, Episode 8)

13.
b: He just wants to see her happy (Season 7, Episode 22)

Chilton

1.
Hartford, Connecticut

2.
A deer (Season 1, Episode 4)

3.
Yellow

4.
The Franklin

ANSWERS

5.
The Puffs (Season 2, Episode 7)

6.
a: The school band (Season 2, Episode 22)

7.
b: 3% (Season 2, Episode 1)

8.
a: Shakespeare, physics and obscure Russian poetry – she tells Henry (Season 2, Episode 2)

9.
Read on her own and listen to her Walkman (Season 2, Episode 7)

10.
The fundraising group – the Chilton Booster Club (Season 2, Episode 7)

11.
Students have signed it in yearbook messages to Rory (Season 3, Episode 21)

LIFE'S SHORT, QUIZ HARD.

Kirk Gleason

Match Kirk's job to the season:

1.
Tow truck operator – Season 5

2.
Wrapping paper salesman – Season 7

3.
Termite inspector – Season 2

4.
Dog walker – Season 4

5.
Mailman – Season 3

6.
Assistant manager at Doose's Market – Season 1

7.
Winter Carnival coordinator – Season 6

8.
b: He is worried about her living alone once Rory has gone to Yale (Season 4, Episode 4)

9.
Lulu (Season 4, Episode 6)

ANSWERS

10.
d: Judas (Season 4, Episode 7)

11.
The woman who seduced the British General and saved Stars Hollow (Season 5, Episode 11)

12.
a: Goldfish (Season 5, Episode 18)

13.
c: Blackjack (Season 5, Episode 18)

Food Glorious Food

1.
b: A Santa burger (Episode 10)

2.
c: Clowns (Episode 18)

3.
d: Blueberry-lemon pancakes, Bananas Foster and Belgian waffles (Season 3, Episode 17)

4.
a: Steak, greens and mashed potato, with lime fantasy supreme for dessert (green jello and Cool Whip) (Season 1, Episode 14)

LIFE'S SHORT, QUIZ HARD.

5.
c: A tassel hat cake, filled with crushed chocolate-covered espresso beans (Season 2, Episode 21)

6.
By crane (Season 3, Episode 18)

7.
a: 'Happy 16th Birthday, Lorelai' (Season 3, Episode 18)

8.
a: Soy pudding (Season 4, Episode 21)

9.
d: Red velvet cake (Season 6, Episode 14)

10.
c: Champagne, vodka, pineapple juice, grenadine and maraschino cherries (Season 6, Episode 7)

Season 6

1.
c: 300 – and one year of probation (Season 6, Episode 1)

2.
a: He and Lorelai are engaged (Season 6, Episode 2)

3.
c: Over $9,000 (Season 6, Episode 3)

ANSWERS

4.
b: She asks them both to be godmothers to her children (Season 6, Episode 4)

5.
a: Lane's (Season 6, Episode 9)

6.
c: A DNA test, to find out if he is her dad (Season 6, Episode 9)

7.
b: Her Yale tuition – so that she doesn't have expectations from her grandparents (Season 6, Episode 10)

8.
Madeline Albright – dream sequence (Season 6, Episode 7)

9.
d: Atlantic City (Season 6, Episode 11)

10.
c: Five months, three weeks and sixteen days (Season 6, Episode 12)

11.
a: April tells Lorelai that her father owns the diner (Season 6, Episode 12)

LIFE'S SHORT, QUIZ HARD.

12.
b: Work in London for a year (Season 6, Episode 15)

13.
a: Write a hit song (Season 6, Episode 17)

14.
c: She kisses Jess (Season 6, Episode 18)

15.
b: The wedding is not going to happen (Season 6, Episode 21)

16.
d: She goes to Christopher's house and says she doesn't want to be alone (Season 6, Episode 22)

Rory and Logan

1.
Ace

2.
Newspapers (Season 5, Episode 6)

3.
b: Richard pretends Logan and Rory are having an arranged wedding (Season 5, Episode 10)

ANSWERS

4.

a: He is not boyfriend material (Season 5, Episode 13)

5.

a: She is outraged, because she is a Gilmore and her family came over on the *Mayflower* (Season 5, Episode 19)

6.

b: An antique sewing box (Season 5, Episode 20)

7.

An Hermès Birkin (Season 6, Episode 6)

8.

3 (Season 6, Episode 16)

9.

It was in an episode of *The Twilight Zone* that they watched together (Season 7, Episode 1)

10.

c: It is mean and judgemental (Season 7, Episode 8)

11.

By helicopter (Season 7, Episode 13)

Yale

1.

b: Her own mattress (Season 4, Episode 2)

LIFE'S SHORT, QUIZ HARD.

2.
a: Roni (Season 4, Episode 2)

3.
She calls her and asks her to come back (Season 4, Episode 2)

4.
Naked Guy (Season 4)

5.
b: 32 (Season 4, Episode 9)

6.
c: She wears red (Harvard's colour) (Season 4, Episode 9)

7.
Swiping cafeteria cards

8.
Marty bartended some of Logan's events (Season 5, Episode 3)

9.
a: Branford College – where her grandfather had also lived when he was at Yale (Season 5, Episode 3)

10.
Paris and Doyle (Season 6, Episode 11)

ANSWERS

11.
They want to buy a building at Yale in her name (Season 6, Episode 21)

12.
English (Season 7, Episode 5)

Paris Geller

1.
a: Assisted suicide (Season 2, Episode 14)

2.
b: That she likes Jess and Rory asked him round to set them up (Season 2, Episode 16)

3.
d: Rory is more likeable (Season 2, Episode 22)

4.
Washington (Season 3, Episode 1)

5.
b: To archive and donate to the university on her demise (Season 3, Episode 17)

6.
a: Eustace (Season 3, Episode 22)

LIFE'S SHORT, QUIZ HARD.

7.
Her life coach, Terrence (Season 4, Episode 1)

8.
He is a professor; Richard introduced them, as he and Asher had been classmates at Yale (Season 4, Episode 9)

9.
Doyle (Season 5, Episode 10)

10.
Krav Maga (Season 5, Episode 15)

11.
c: Rory was elected editor of the *Yale Daily News* (Season 6, Episode 14)

12.
c: 8 (Season 7, Episode 19)

Sookie St. James
1.
d: Lorelai and Jackson's cousin Rune (Season 1, Episode 11)

2.
a: Clyde (Season 2, Episode 4)

ANSWERS

3.
Nick Offerman (Season 4, Episode 7)

4.
b: Kirk (Season 2, Episode 13)

5.
c: There is a large cut at the back (Season 3, Episode 10)

6.
c: He wants four children in four years (Season 3, Episode 7)

7.
He deep-fries the turkey and then deep-fries anything else he can get his hands on (Season 3, Episode 9)

8.
He only orders iced tea (Season 5, Episode 6)

9.
a: Billy Joel (Season 5, Episode 6)

10.
b: During the Festival of Living Pictures, while Lorelai is trying to pose without moving (Season 4, Episode 7)

11.
Davey and Martha

LIFE'S SHORT, QUIZ HARD.

Season 7

1.
c: She slept with Christopher (Season 7, Episode 1)

2.
b: She is pregnant (Season 7, Episode 3)

3.
a: They come to pick her up from the police station together – she is arrested for talking on a cell phone while driving (Season 7, Episode 4)

4.
b: The whole of the *Yale Daily News* staff (Season 7, Episode 6)

5.
a: They got a very expensive dog licence (Season 7, Episode 8)

6.
c: He is going to court to get shared custody of April (Season 7, Episode 11)

7.
d: Everything she and Rory need to do to get a job, fellowship or into grad school (Season 7, Episode 12)

ANSWERS

8.
Krysten Ritter (Season 7, Episode 4)

9.
a: She thinks Jackson got a vasectomy (Season 7, Episode 12)

10.
d: He has a heart attack (Season 7, Episode 12)

11.
c: Wheeled in her bed (she is on bedrest with the twins) (Season 7, Episode 16)

12.
a: In the Hale Bale Maze (Season 7, Episode 18)

13.
At her graduation party, hosted at her grandparents' (Season 7, Episode 21)

14.
b: Barack Obama (Season 7, Episode 22)

15.
b: At Rory's going away party – organised by Luke and Sookie (Season 7, Episode 22)

16.
c: Luke's Diner (Season 7, Episode 22)

LIFE'S SHORT, QUIZ HARD.

Random Dates

1.
Tristan (Season 1, Episode 17)

2.
b: In her business class (Season 2, Episode 9)

3.
Kirk (Season 3, Episode 2)

4.
a: Alex

5.
Literature class (Season 4, Episode 5)

6.
Jon Hamm, before *Mad Men* (Season 3, Episode 5)

7.
Digger (Season 4, Episode 6)

8.
A supermarket

9.
c: A private investigator (Paluso) hired by Jason's father (Season 4, Episode 18)

ANSWERS

10.
b: He acts like he doesn't know her (Season 7)

Extra-Curricular

1.
Paris

2.
Doyle

3.
c: A ballerina (Season 4, Episode 8)

4.
A hat made out of newspaper (Season 4, Episode 10)

5.
a: So she doesn't need to learn their names (Season 6, Episode 12)

6.
d: The newspaper went to press with a blank photo in the sports page (Season 6, Episode 13)

7.
Rory (Season 6, Episode 14)

LIFE'S SHORT, QUIZ HARD.

8.
He takes credit for her becoming editor of the *Yale Daily News* (Season 6, Episode 21)

9.
b: Helps keep Logan on the right career path (Season 7, Episode 15)

10.
New York Times

11.
Gorilla

12.
b: No photos, names or defining physical characteristics (Season 5, Episode 7)

13.
In Omnia Paratus, 'Ready for All Things' (Season 5, Episode 7)

14.
Event planning

15.
Costa Rica (Season 6, Episode 19)

ANSWERS

Luke Danes

1.
Nicole

2.
b: Their love of *Bewitched* (Season 4, Episode 19)

3.
a: Dean – They fight in the street (Season 1, Episode 17)
b: Jess – Luke pushes him into a lake (Season 2, Episode 5)
e: Christopher – Luke punches him in the face (Season 7, Episode 2)

4.
He wants to buy it

5.
It is the anniversary of his father's death (Season 5, Episode 10)

6.
a: A pearl necklace (that was his mother's) (Season 6, Episode 7)

7.
Anna Nardini (Season 6, Episode 9)

8.
b: 2 months (Season 6, Episode 12)

LIFE'S SHORT, QUIZ HARD.

9.
b: Hagrid (Season 6, Episode 20)

10.
a: Lorelai planned it (Season 6, Episode 20)

11.
c: Punches Christopher in the face (Season 7, Episode 2)

12.
a: Swimming (Season 7, Episode 5)

13.
To be nearer her mother (Season 7, Episode 9)

Friday Night Dinners
b: Rory and Dean's anniversary (Season 1, Episode 16)
d: Telling Dean about the car accident with Jess (Season 2, Episode 20)
f: Having a cold (Season 4, Episode 15)
h: Rory meeting Sherry (Season 2, Episode 14)
j: Sherry going into labour (Season 3, Episode 13)

Christopher Hayden
1.
c: An internet startup (Season 1, Episode 1)

ANSWERS

2.
b: An *Oxford English Dictionary* (Season 1, Episode 15)

3.
Straub and Francine (Season 1, Episode 15)

4.
She takes a job in Paris (Season 5, Episode 6)

5.
Mädchen Amick, who also played Sherry in *Twin Peaks*

6.
d: His father was sick and it made him want to improve his relationship with her

7.
d: His grandfather (Season 6, Episode 10)

8.
c: A Sidekick (Season 6, Episode 19)

9.
b: By letter (Season 7, Episode 5)

***A Year in the Life*, 'Winter'**

1.
London

LIFE'S SHORT, QUIZ HARD.

2.
b: Princess Charlotte-branded iced-tea spoons

3.
a: Brooklyn

4.
c: 2 years

5.
Tap

6.
a: Dinerluke
b: DINERDANES321

7.
Rory's *New Yorker* article

8.
c: Roy Choi

9.
A year

10.
d: The Carpenters

11.
b: 32

ANSWERS

12.
It covers the whole wall

13.
Jason Stiles (Digger)

14.
Twin Peaks

15.
b: 4 months

16.
Paris Geller

17.
a: 'What happens in Vegas, stays in Vegas'

18.
Screenwriter

19.
b: 50 years

20.
c: Sees a therapist

LIFE'S SHORT, QUIZ HARD.

A Year in the Life, 'Spring'

1.
Mr Kim

2.
15

3.
b: Liza Minnelli's 70th birthday

4.
a: Matthew McConaughey
b: Jessica Chastain

5.
b: 10

6.
At her friend Didi's

7.
c: The Ivy

8.
Odette

9.
Eraserhead

ANSWERS

10.
d: She doesn't do email

11.
She is going to a Chilton alumni event

12.
Richard left him money to extend and franchise his diner

13.
c: $100,000

14.
a: Roommates with benefits

15.
Tristan

16.
Nothing

17.
People who wait in lines in New York

18.
c: A cro-dough-cake

19.
d: A Wookie

LIFE'S SHORT, QUIZ HARD.

20.
c: 3 – one for work, one for family and one for friends

A Year in the Life, 'Summer'

1.
c: 22

2.
She will have to stay in a hotel as Odette has moved in

3.
Thirty-year-olds who have moved back into their parents' homes in Stars Hollow

4.
b: 89

5.
d: Whittling

6.
Editor of the *Stars Hollow Gazette*

7.
Zach and Lane

8.
b: Taylor is on his way, so all patrons and tables have to be hidden out of sight

ANSWERS

9.
a: The poem

10.
d: The W Hotel in New York (he needs more money to support his future family with Frederick)

11.
Bernie Roundbottom

12.
b: Paul Thomas Anderson

13.
Michael Bay

14.
a: 'I Feel the Earth Move'

15.
c: Lucy in *You're a Good Man, Charlie Brown*

16.
c: The fifth

17.
There are single quotation marks instead of double quotation marks

LIFE'S SHORT, QUIZ HARD.

18.
Rory and Lorelai's story

19.
It's Lorelai's life

20.
d: Hike the Pacific West Trail from *Wild*

A Year in the Life, 'Fall'

1.
Those who are following the book or movie

2.
c: 'Kick up a rumpus'

3.
The Wi-Fi password

4.
He buys it and changes the music to only songs by Rosemary Clooney.

5.
a: His family house in Maine – bought to annoy Martha Stewart

6.
She doesn't have her permit

ANSWERS

7.
Her grandfather's study

8.
c: Harvest Festival

9.
b: He might be too exhausted to look for wife number five

10.
Kiefer Sutherland

11.
d: The Sandcastle

12.
To buy an annex for the Inn

13.
Two weeks in Nantucket in the summer and one week at Christmas

14.
a: Wedding cakes

15.
She had cut the top of her finger off

16.
c: If he minds being in her book

LIFE'S SHORT, QUIZ HARD.

17.
Rory should drop the 'The'

18.
c: The song they first danced to (at Luke's sister's wedding): 'Reflecting Light' by Sam Phillips

19.
He sends her a text message

20.
'Mom, I'm pregnant'